A Manual for American Servicemen in the Arab Middle East

A Manual for American Servicemen in the Arab Middle East

Using Cultural Understanding to Defeat Adversaries and Win the Peace

Lt. Col. William D. Wunderle

Skyhorse Publishing

Skyhorse Publishing books may be purchased in bulk at special discounts for sales promotion, corporate gifts, fund raising, or educational purposes. Special editions can also be created to specifications. For details, contact? Special Sales Department, Skyhorse Publishing, 555 Eighth Avenue, Suite 903, New York, NY 10018 or info@skyhorsepublishing.com.

www.skyhorsepublishing.com

Library of Congress Cataloging-in-Publication Data

Wunderle, William D., 1962–
    A manual for American servicemen in the Arab Middle East : using cultural understanding to defeat adversaries and win the peace / William D. Wunderle.
    p. cm.
Includes bibliographical references and index.
ISBN-13: 978-1-60239-277-9 (pbk. : alk. paper)
ISBN-10: 1-60239-277-3 (pbk. : alk. paper)
1. United States—Armed Forces—Foreign service—Middle East—Handbooks, manuals, etc. 2. Arab countries—Social life and customs. 3. National characteristics, Arab. 4. National characteristics, Iraqi. 5. Cultural awareness—Study and teaching—United States. I. Title.

UA26.A2W36 2008
306.0917'4927—dc22   2007051243

10 9 8 7 6 5 4 3 2 1

Printed in Canada

Contents

Page

Figures

Tables

Preface

Conducting the Long War and projecting United States influence around the world has meant that an increasing number of US diplomats and military personnel have been assigned to locations across the globe, some of which have not previously had a significant US presence. In the current security environment, understanding foreign cultures and societies has become a national priority. Cultural understanding is necessary both to defeat culturally dissimilar adversaries and to work successfully with allies of different cultures. An understanding of Islamic cultures is particularly important, as indicated by recent experiences in Iraq, Afghanistan, and Somalia. This document defines a way in which US military leaders can prepare for and conduct military operations through the lens of "cultural awareness." It provides a method for helping military commanders, staff, and trainers to successfully engage in any type of operation with an emphasis on post-conflict stability operations. The document also suggests modifications to the traditional intelligence preparation of the battlefield (IPB) and military decisionmaking processes (MDMP) in order to address the analytical difficulties posed by the conduct of military operations within and among different cultures.

This research was initially undertaken to support military training conducted at the Joint Readiness Training Center (JRTC) and the National Training Center (NTC) and has since informed studies being conducted within the RAND Corporation and the Institute for Creative Technologies as well as a number of projects, conferences, and training conducted throughout the Department of Defense (DoD), Department of State (DoS), and miscellaneous intelligence agencies.

This study will be of interest to servicemen, civilians, contractors, and intelligence community personnel planning for or conducting operations in Arab and Middle East countries. It will also be of interest to any armed forces, law enforcement, security, or intelligence community personnel that need to assess the intentions, motivations, and decisionmaking style of persons from non-US cultures.

Acknowledgments

This book is not the work of an individual, but the result of many who provided information, assistance, and guidance throughout the research effort that led to the successful publication of this book. From the RAND Corporation, I would like to extend a special note of thanks to Kristin Leuschner, who was able to take my initial briefing slides and disparate notes, and combine them into a well-formulated, congruent document while offering valuable suggestions on how it could be improved, and Tom Szayna for his professional advice, mentorship, and tireless efforts in reviewing this research as it progressed.

I also appreciate receiving input from Bruce Hoffman, Eric Larson, and Scott Gerwher, who each provided professional advice, friendship, and an initial review of this research, the staff of the Combat Studies Institute at Fort Leavenworth, Kansas, the Defense Language Institute Foreign Language Center, and Maj Ben Connable of the USMC Cultural Awareness Working Group. There are also a number of my Arab and Islamic friends and colleagues who were instrumental in verifying this research. At their request, I have not included their names in this report. I am additionally indebted to the formal reviewers of this project for their constructive criticism and comments.

Finally, I want thank my wife, Vicki, a Middle East specialist in her own right, who provided valuable research assistance, editorial comments, and reviews—this work would not have been possible without her support. This book is dedicated to my daughter Christine and my son Will; without their years of patience, understanding, and support for a father in the military, this book could not have been written. Please note that all omissions or mistakes are the sole responsibility of this author.

Chapter 1

Introduction

Projection of United States (US) influence around the world has brought an increasing number of US military forces into foreign lands. As recent experiences in Iraq, Afghanistan, Somalia, and other locations demonstrate, an understanding of foreign cultures and societies has become a national priority. Military leaders have long understood that knowledge of the adversary is critical to operational success. Cultural awareness is an increasingly important component of this knowledge; indeed, the more unconventional the adversary (and the more it diverges from US cultural norms), the more important it is for the US military to understand the adversary's society and underlying cultural dynamics as a means of ensuring operational success. Cultural awareness can reduce battlefield friction and the fog of war. It can improve the military's ability to accomplish its mission by providing insight into the intent of the groups in the battlespace, thus allowing military leaders to outthink and outmaneuver them. An understanding of cultures and societies is also critical to postconflict stability and support operations (SASO), peacekeeping, and nation-building, all of which require close and sometimes long-term interaction between people of other cultures and US soldiers. In addition, the success of US military operations calls for American soldiers to become experts in not only the culture of their adversaries, but also in the cultures of their allies, civilian counterparts, nongovernmental organizations (NGOs), international organizations, and others.

Despite the growing awareness among national leaders of the need to include cultural awareness as part of military operations, battle preparations as well as military training and doctrine neglect the role of culture and religion. Cultural awareness is not currently included as part of foreign language training, and the cultural training provided to soldiers prior to deployment tends to be overly simplistic, typically focusing on lists of do's and don'ts without providing a context for cultural understanding. Current US joint doctrine does not stress consideration of any type of cultural awareness and competence factors during the deliberate planning process. Intelligence gathering also neglects culture.

This document addresses these gaps by presenting a methodology to help members of the US Armed Forces understand foreign cultures, including the ways culture can influence how people think and act. In addition, it provides a conceptual model that can be applied in understanding any culture and illustrates the use of this model with a Middle Eastern case study, including examples from Iraq.

Why Culture Matters

Cultural factors have been a critical, yet mostly unexamined, aspect of missions conducted in Africa and the Middle East since the end of the first Gulf War in 1991. Cultural factors played an important, but usually unacknowledged, role in shaping the scope of the United States' humanitarian intervention in Somalia during the 1990s.[1] Today, with much of the US military either in Iraq, returning from Iraq, or getting ready to go to Iraq, cultural awareness seems to be almost a basic requirement for success on the battlefield (including psychological operations, information and influence operations, effects-based operations, strategic communications, and civil affairs) and in postconflict operations. Lessons from recent and ongoing operations have demonstrated the need for improved cultural knowledge and foreign language capability among US forces, with an emphasis on languages reflective of the post-Cold War threat. (These include Albanian, Arabic, Chinese, Dari, Hindi, Kurdish, Pashto, Persian-Farsi, Russian, Serbian-Croatian, Turkish, and Urdu.)[2] Cultural awareness could become even more important in the future due to the persistence of nationalism and social traditionalism in some regions of the world and the potential for continuing cultural and religious tensions.

The following examples illustrate what can happen when military operations do *not* consider cultural awareness.

A lack of cultural awareness among American forces has led to an increase in animosity among many Iraqis and contributed to a negative image of the US military. American forces in Iraq have engaged in the practice of destroying the houses of suspected insurgents without judicial due process. Such actions have resonated among the local population due to similar tactics used by the Israeli military in the occupied territories of the Gaza Strip and the West Bank. Soldiers have also shown ignorance of Islamic religious practice. For example, "Iraqis arrested by US troops have had their heads forced to the ground, a position forbidden by Islam except during prayers. This action offends detainees as well as bystanders. . . . the military has enough to worry about without alienating the local population."[3] Tactics such as these might bestow short-term tactical advantages and might appear to be effective measures, but can undermine the long-term US goals for building stability in the region.

Difficulty in understanding the interrelationship between religion and politics has contributed to power imbalances in Iraq. A failure to understand the dynamics of tribalism and the role of tribal leaders (who are often competing with other governing and administrative structures such as town councils and local police), has led some American units to disproportionately empower tribal structures, and others to virtually ignore them. In addition, American forces entering Iraq with Kuwaiti translators encountered an unexpected negative Iraqi response due to animosity between Iraqis and Kuwaitis, of which many Americans were unaware. Tribal rivalries have also come into play due to the need for US forces to rely heavily on locally hired translators, some of whom may cause interference with US objectives and operations or even gain a disproportionate influence.[4]

A lack of cultural awareness appears to have affected military operations. A commander from 3d Infantry Division observed: "I had perfect situational awareness. What I lacked was cultural awareness. I knew where every enemy tank was dug in on the outskirts of Tallil. Only problem was, my soldiers had to fight fanatics charging on foot or in pickups and firing AK47s and RPGs. Great technical intelligence. . . . Wrong enemy."[5]

Understanding an adversary requires more than intelligence from three-letter agencies and satellite photos; it requires an understanding of their interests, habits, intentions, beliefs, social organizations, and political symbols—in other words, their culture. An American soldier can liken culture to a minefield: dangerous ground that, if not breached, must be navigated with caution, understanding, and respect. Cultural interpretation, competence, and adaptation are prerequisites for achieving a win-win relationship in any military operation. Operational commanders who do not consider the role of culture during mission planning and execution invite unintended and unforeseen consequences, and even mission failure.[6]

Cultural Awareness in Current Military Training and Doctrine

There is a growing recognition of the need for cultural awareness in US military battle preparations, training, and doctrine. In a letter to Secretary of Defense Donald Rumsfeld dated 21 October 2003, Congressman Ike Skelton, the ranking Democrat on the House Armed Services Committee, wrote: "[If] we had better understood the Iraqi culture and mindset, our war plans would have been even better than they were, [and] the plan for the post-war period and all of its challenges would have been far better. . . . we must improve our cultural awareness . . . to inform the policy process. Our policies would benefit from this not only in Iraq, but . . . elsewhere, where we will have long-term strategic relationships and potential military challenges for many years to come." In response, Secretary Rumsfeld released a memorandum stating that "foreign language skill and regional expertise are essential enabling capabilities for DOD activities in the transition to and from hostilities." This memorandum further stipulates that not only will the Secretaries of the military departments reshape the forces to "provide stabilization and reconstruction capabilities . . . capable of operating in a range of cultures and languages," but further tasks the Under Secretary of Defense for Personnel and Readiness (USD(P&R)) to develop metrics to evaluate and report individual and unit capabilities and readiness in the areas of foreign language speakers and personnel with regional and cultural expertise.[7]

In a recent self-assessment, the Department of Defense (DOD) rated itself as "inadequate" in its culture and language preparation to conduct missions throughout the spectrum of operations.[8] In a similar assessment conducted by the combatant commands, Pacific Command (PACOM) rated itself as "generally inadequate," while European Command (EUCOM) and Central Command (CENTCOM) each rated itself as "inadequate" in knowledge of societal, cultural, tribal structure, economy, infrastructure, evolving threats, and number of in-house specialists in its respective area of responsibility (AOR).[9]

Lessons from recent operations indicate that improvements are needed in "institutional preparation in language, as well as political, ideological, and cultural training."[10] At the Defense Language Institute Foreign Language Center (DLI-FLC),[11] the US military's premier language-training center, culture is not currently part of the curriculum despite clear guidance from the Defense Foreign Language Program as described by the National Security Agency (NSA) and the Defense Intelligence Agency (DIA).[12] Some DLIFLC faculty feel that teaching culture as part of language training is too difficult or too controversial. It has sometimes been considered too "politically sensitive and there are too many conflicting or extremist views which preclude anything beyond a cursory look at culture."[13]

Too often, the cultural training that does exist is overly simplistic, focusing mostly on points of etiquette, such as not using the left hand or showing the bottoms of the feet.[14] While these behavioral guidelines can be useful, they do not go nearly far enough, nor do they provide soldiers with an adequate understanding of the reasons behind these directives. Indeed, in some cases, soldiers trying to follow these rules focus more on avoiding offending someone than they do on their mission.

Moreover, behavioral guidelines do not assist soldiers in developing the critical thinking skills needed to understand how culture might influence an operation. According to United States Marine Corps (USMC) research,[15] soldiers and leaders need to be able to use their understanding of other cultures to answer questions such as:

* What is my adversary thinking and why?
* What are my friends thinking and why?
* What will they do if I take action X and why?
* How are cultural factors influencing my operations?
* How can I make others do what I want them to do?

Soldiers need cultural knowledge that can be strategically applied when needed.

Thorough guidelines for developing cultural awareness are missing from training and doctrine. Programs for training cultural awareness are not found in any US military training manual or doctrinal publication, and only a few civilian publications come close to meeting the cultural awareness training needs of American soldiers operating overseas.[16] While country studies and other textbook-like materials and briefings provide useful means of obtaining basic facts and data on a particular country or region, they are not sufficient to describe the relevant cultural aspects of particular societies. Current US joint doctrine does not stress consideration of any type of cultural awareness and competence factors during the deliberate planning process. Cultural factors addressed in joint doctrine typically occur in reference to working with coalition partners and not to the ways in which cultural factors could affect enemy reaction and impact the selected course of action (COA).[17] Although US joint doctrine acknowledges that cultural differences among coalition partners may impact the mission, it does not consider the impact of culture on internal mission planning. Even today, there is limited US doctrine on how to advise and train foreign forces. This is significant given the priority and importance of training Iraqi security forces and the fact that the training of foreign forces differs significantly from the training provided to US forces. Furthermore, current US joint doctrine does not provide commanders with a comprehensive and structured approach for incorporating cultural considerations into the operational planning process. Such an approach is necessary to mitigate possible negative impacts on plan execution and operational success.

Purpose and Organization

As this introduction has suggested, military commanders and staffs at all levels must address cultural awareness as an important operational planning factor to eliminate errors that may lead to unforeseen consequences and ultimately mission failure. Culture must become a formal part of soldiers' training. This document presents recommendations for incorporating a cultural framework into military planning, training, and doctrine and presents a conceptual model to help members of the US Armed Forces understand foreign cultures and the ways culture can influence peoples' thoughts and actions.

Because of the importance of Iraq and Middle Eastern culture in the current security environment, the case study creates a sort of primer on Middle Eastern culture. This case study can be used as a cross-cultural guide for members of the US Armed Forces who are living in an Arab country, those who may be deployed to an Arab country, those who may encounter Arabs, and those who are interested in the behaviors of Arabs. The conceptual framework and cultural analyses presented are drawn from relevant scholarly literature and personal observations and experience. The section on Middle Eastern culture also draws on interviews and discussions with dozens of native Arabs from throughout the Middle East and North Africa.[18]

Any attempt to describe the motives and values of an entire population is risky because it can lead to generalizations that are not always true. An understanding of culture involves the perspectives and interpretations of the observer, which can cause some traits and behaviors to be emphasized over others.[19] Do not interpret anything in this document as a value judgment—this document aims to describe cultural differences, not to judge them.

The remainder of this document is organized in four chapters. Chapter 2 presents a conceptual framework for developing cultural awareness, and chapter 3 applies this framework to Middle Eastern culture, including a discussion of Iraq. Chapter 4 discusses ways to integrate cultural awareness into training and doctrine, and chapter 5 presents the summary and conclusion.

Notes

1. The implications of cultural factors for US operations in Somalia are discussed in appendix D. While the primary focus of this manuscript is on the Middle East in general and Iraq specifically, US and UN operations in Somalia provide additional insights into the role of cultural awareness.

2. Charles S. Abell, "Testimony Before the House Armed Services Committee Subcommittee on Total Force," United States House of Representatives, 24 March 2004.

3. Ike Skelton and Jim Cooper, "You're Not from Around Here, Are You?" *Joint Forces Quarterly*, vol. 36, December 2004, 12–16.

4. Center for Army Lessons Learned (CALL), "Chapter 2: Civil Military Operations—Civil Affairs, Topic C: Cultural Issues in Iraq," in *Operation Iraqi Freedom (OIF)*, CAAT II Initial Impressions Report (IIR) No. 04-13 (Fort Leavenworth, KS: Center for Army Lessons Learned, May 2004).

5. Steve Israel and Robert Scales, "Iraq Proves It: Military Needs Better Intel," *New York Daily News*, 7 January 2004.

6. Calvin F. Swain, Jr., *The Operational Planning Factors of Culture and Religion* (Newport, RI: US Naval War College, 13 May 2003), 1.

7. Secretary of Defense Memorandum, "Defense Capabilities to and from Hostilities," 8 October 2004. Other current legislation and policies governing this issue include Department of Defense, "Military Support for Stability, Security, Transition, and Reconstruction (SSTR) Operations," Directive Number 3000.05, 28 November 2005; Under Secretary of Defense for Personnel and Readiness Memorandum on "Defense Language Institute Abbreviated Course," 27 October 2003, calls for the Defense Language Institute Foreign Language Center (DLIFLC) to develop a compressed course to be administered through Mobile Training Teams (MTTs) to unit installations and provide on-site training; Under Secretary of Defense for Personnel and Readiness Statement of Work number DAS W01-03-T-0124 seeks to transform the way language is valued, developed, and employed within the Department of Defense; Assistant Secretaries of the Army, Navy, and Air Force Memorandum on "Defense Language Transformation" (undated) recommends consultation with combatant commanders to identify real-world problems experienced as a result of scarce knowledge among military personnel of foreign languages and cultures; DA G-3 message on "Defense Language Institute Abbreviated Arabic Course," November 2003, seeks input from all the services on their need for cultural familiarization and foreign language training; and Chairman, Joint Chiefs of Staff Memorandum on "Defense Language Institute Abbreviated Course," 5 December 2003, documents the service's agreement that a language and culture course is warranted.

8. Defense Science Board 2004 Summer Study, "Transition to and from Hostilities," September 2004, 12.

9. Ibid., 25.

10. CALL (2004).

11. With over 1,300 faculty and 3,800 students, the Defense Language Institute Foreign Language Center (DLIFLC) is the world's largest foreign language school and the military's primary source of language instruction. DLIFLC has more faculty teaching DOD's five highest enrollment languages than all US students graduating in those languages nationwide. It is an institution whose product—a language qualified graduate—is critical to global US military operations.

12. Kenneth L. Sampson, "Instilling Passion for Language: Strategies and Techniques," in *Dialog on Language Instruction*, vol. 13, nos. 1 and 2 (Presidio of Monterey: Defense Language Institute Foreign Language Center, 1999), 74.

13. Based on correspondence between a senior administrator at DLIFLC and the author.

14. Even today, after years of experience in Afghanistan and Iraq, this type of cultural training is still prevalent in the US Army's training centers. See Office of the Deputy Chief of Staff for Intelligence, "Arab Cultural Awareness: 58 Fact Sheets," TRADOC DCSINT Handbook No. 2 (Fort Leavenworth, KS: US Army Training and Doctrine Command, 7 February 2005).

15. Ben Connable and Art Speyer, "Cultural Awareness for Military Operations," *Concepts and Proposals: USMC Cultural Awareness Working Group* (HQMC and MCIA, February 2005).

16. For example, Glen Fisher, *Mindsets: The Role of Culture and Perception in International Relations*, 2d edition (Yarmouth, ME: Intercultural Press, Inc., 1997); Margaret K. (Omar) Nydell, *Understanding Arabs: A Guide for Westerners,* 3d edition (Yarmouth, ME: Intercultural Press, Inc., 2002); and Raphael Patai, *The Arab Mind* (Hatherleigh Press, May 2002) are three books that military leaders at all levels might consult before deploying to the Middle East.

17. See Appendix A, "Cultural Factors in US Joint and Army Doctrine."

18. These interviews took place over a number of years through the author's personal and professional contacts. The evidence is based on casual conversation and much of the evidence is anecdotal.

19. Nydell (2002), x–xii.

Chapter 2

A Conceptual Model for Understanding Culture

This chapter provides formal definitions of culture and cultural awareness and then presents a three-part conceptual model to address cultural awareness in military operations. Culture might be considered the "human terrain" of warfare, and it is a key terrain. Understanding and being able to apply cultural concepts on the battlefield can make or break mission accomplishment. Success on the battlefield—and in peacekeeping, nationbuilding, and other noncombat operations—results from the ability of leaders to understand the human terrain and to think and adapt faster than the enemy, and from the ability of soldiers to make their way successfully in an environment of uncertainty, ambiguity, and unfamiliarity.[1]

Culture and Cultural Awareness Defined

The formal definitions of the terms "culture" and "cultural awareness" follow:

Culture: A shared set of traditions, belief systems, and behaviors.[2] Culture is shaped by many factors, including history, religion, ethnic identity, language, and nationality. Culture evolves in response to various pressures and influences and is learned through socialization; it is not inherent. In short, a culture provides a lens through which its members see and understand the world.

In a military context, think of culture as simply another element of terrain, parallel to geographic terrain. Just as a hill or saddle affect a soldier's ability to maneuver, so can religion, perceptions, and language help military planners find centers of gravity and critical vulnerabilities, and assist in campaign planning and the proper allocation of resources.

Cultural Awareness: The ability to recognize and understand the effects of culture on people's values and behaviors. In the military context, cultural awareness can be defined as the "cognizance of cultural terrain for military operations and the connections between culture and warfighting."[3] Cultural awareness implies an understanding of the need to consider cultural terrain in military operations, a knowledge of which cultural factors are important for a given situation and why, and a specified level of understanding for a target culture.

At an elementary level, cultural awareness is information, the meaning humans assign to what they know about a culture. A principal task involved in acquiring cultural awareness is to collect cultural information and transform it by adding progressively greater meaning as understanding deepens.

Levels of understanding can be conceptualized as a kind of "cognitive hierarchy":[4]

- *Data.* Data are the lowest level of information on the cognitive hierarchy. Data consist of unprocessed signals communicated between any nodes in an information system, or sensings from the environment detected through human, mechanical, or electronic means.
- *Information.* In the context of the cognitive hierarchy, information is data that have been processed to provide further meaning.
- *Knowledge.* In the context of the cognitive hierarchy, knowledge is information analyzed to provide meaning and value, or evaluated as to implications for the operation.
- *Understanding.* In the context of the cognitive hierarchy, understanding is knowledge that has been synthesized and had judgment applied to it in a specific situation to allow for comprehension of a situation's inner relationships.

To understand and apply cultural awareness to a military context, use the levels in the cognitive hierarchy. The pyramid in figure 1 is a graphic representation of cultural awareness applied to the cognitive hierarchy.[5] Because information gives structure and shape to military operations and the battlespace, such a model of cultural awareness can be used as a framework for training, planning, and executing military operations. Commanders and staffs can then give meaning to and gain understanding of the events and conditions in which they make decisions and conduct operations.

Figure 1 illustrates the point that cultural awareness is not a "do/don't do" kind of knowledge, but one that provides various levels of capabilities for understanding cultures (through a cultural lens) and applying one's understanding to the situation at hand. These capabilities are conceptualized as levels in the pyramid, because military personnel with different levels and types of responsibilities (commanders versus soldiers) require different levels of cultural awareness. An explanation of the levels follows:

- *Cultural consideration* ("how and why") is the incorporation of generic cultural concepts in common military training—knowing how and why to study culture and where to find cultural factors and expertise.
- *Cultural knowledge* (specific training) is exposure to the recent history of a target culture. It includes basic cultural issues such as significant groups, actors, leaders, and dynamics, as well as cultural niceties and survival language skills.
- *Cultural understanding* (advanced training) refers to a deeper awareness of the specific culture that allows general insight into thought processes, motivating factors, and other issues that directly support the military decisionmaking process.

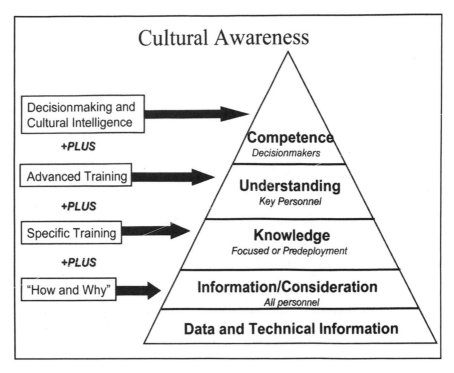

Figure 1. Cultural awareness pyramid.

- *Cultural competence* (decision-making and cultural intelligence) is the fusion of cultural understanding with cultural intelligence that allows focused insight into military planning and decision-making for current and future military operations.[6] Cultural competence implies insight into the intentions of specific actors and groups. (Chapter 4 further develops this concept.)

It is important to note that there is no single solution to apply at all echelons—one "size" of cultural awareness does not fit all. The level of understanding required at different echelons will vary according to the specific needs of the mission.

A Conceptual Model for Developing Cultural Awareness

Now that key definitions have been established, figure 2 shows a model for understanding culture and developing cultural awareness.[7]

The three main components that define culture are cultural influences, cultural variations, and cultural manifestations. Understanding each of these is important to the development of cultural awareness.

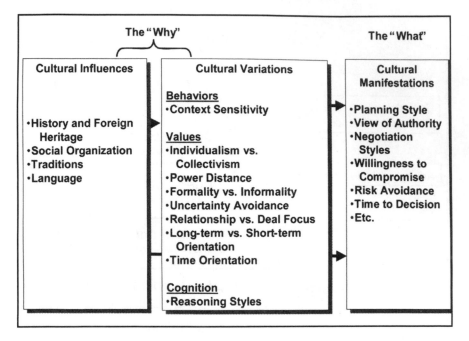

Figure 2. Taxonomy of culture.

- Cultural influences are major social or institutional factors, such as heritage, religion, traditions, and language that bind people together. Of particular importance is a culture's heritage or history, which can be critical in defining the culture's ethnic and national identity. What is most critical in terms of influence is typically not the factual history of a country or region, but the group's collective memory and interpretation of that past. This becomes an inherited remembrance that is passed from one generation to the next.
- Cultural variations include styles of behavior, values, and ways of thinking that are common to a culture. Behaviors are the outward, observable artifacts of a culture. They consist of the language, social rules, customs, structures, and institutions of a given culture. Values are principles that members of a culture use to evaluate alternatives or consequences in decisionmaking. Ways of thinking, or cognition, refer to preference-based strategies and processes that inform decisionmaking, perceptions, and knowledge representation in a given culture. It is "the mental process of knowing, including aspects such as awareness, perception, reasoning, and judgment."[8]
- Cultural manifestations are the concrete displays of a culture's thought and behavior, including its members' view of authority, negotiation

style, willingness to compromise, embracing of risk, and other characteristics.

In a sense, cultural influences and variations explain *why* the culture is the way it is. Cultural manifestations, on the other hand, refer to *what* one encounters in the culture. These concepts are discussed in more detail below.

Cultural Influences

Embedded in larger networks of social structures and historical forces, cultures help shape concrete behaviors and thought processes. As such, cultural influences such as religion or history can help define a culture and establish a context for understanding a culture whether or not every individual in the culture is personally affected by these influences.

The history and foreign heritage of a given area may provide a worldview that reflects and supports the social, political, and economic organization, which can offer some guidance to the values that are likely to characterize the cultures within that region. Likewise, religion addresses not only the formal structure of religions within a culture, but also the role that religion and spirituality play in a culture. The nature of religious beliefs within a culture reflects and supports social structures and cultural values.[9]

Note that these influences are not absolute, but instead reflect tendencies within cultures. These characteristics are generalizations that are not applicable to all community members, but nonetheless can influence the way people think and behave. Within any given culture, there is likely to be variation between individuals in the weight these influences have (for example, some individuals may be very nationalistic, others may be less so).

Cultural Variations

Social science researchers have identified a set of universal traits that can define variations within a culture. The researchers further divide cultural variations into three broad categories: behaviors, values, and cognition.[10]

Behaviors

Behaviors are the outward, observable artifacts of a culture. They consist of the language, social rules, customs, structures, and institutions of a given culture and include:

- Languages, customs, dress, religion.
- Language styles, including the degree of context sensitivity; that is, the extent to which language emphasizes surrounding circumstances (or context) and makes use of body language.
- Personal space or the physical region or space around an individual within which it is considered taboo (to varying degrees) for another individual to enter.

The following is a detailed discussion of the latter two concepts.

Context Sensitivity. Benjamin Whorf, a linguistic anthropologist at Yale University in the 1930s, argued that the content of a language is directly related to the content of a culture and the structure of a language is directly related to the structure of a culture.[11] The result of this process is many different views by speakers of different languages. Language is not simply a way of voicing ideas, but the very thing that shapes those ideas. In other words, a person cannot think outside the confines of his or her language, and the language used can influence the way a person sees the world. Conversely, the way a person sees the world can also influence the kind of language he or she uses. Understanding of a particular culture, therefore, requires an understanding of the context in which that group communicates.

There are two types of communication: low-context and high-context. In low-context communications, the meaning of what is said is, for the most part, explicit in the words spoken—words alone provide most of the meaning. While there can be some variation in the meaning of a particular phrase or sentence, this variation does not range widely according to context. In high-context communications, however, meaning is implicit rather than explicit in the language. This means that words can be understood only within a given situation or context, and that nonverbal communications take on greater importance in interpreting what is meant. For example, the Arabic language is a high-context language, which means that what is "not said" may be more important than what is said. Context sensitivity is important because the surrounding circumstances determine the meaning of the words spoken. Figure 3 categorizes various cultures according to the level of context sensitivity inherent to the culture's language.

Personal Space. The importance of body language, especially the role of gestures and eye contact, also varies among cultures. Social scientists conclude that only about 7 percent of the emotional meaning of a message is communicated by the words that are spoken, while 38 percent of the meaning is paralinguistic (in the way the words are said), and 55 percent of the meaning is delivered by the use of gestures, posture, and facial expressions.[12] In cultures where body language plays a key role, feelings and emotional responses are generally based not so much on what another person *says*, but on what another person *does*.

Values

Values are the principles for evaluating alternatives or consequences in decisionmaking and constitute the base judgments of what is considered good or bad within a culture.[13] These values can be used to provide a lens through which an individual of a particular culture sees the world.

Geert Hofstede, an influential theorist on the practical aspects of cultural differences at the national level, describes five dimensions through which all

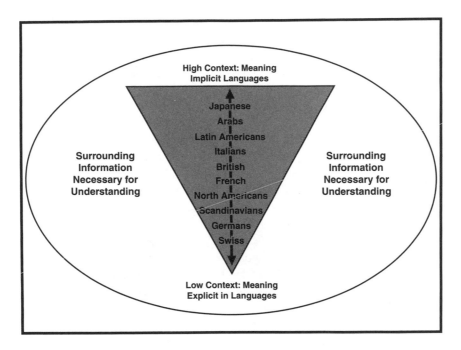

Figure 3. Levels of context sensitivity inherent to various cultures.

cultures can be described.[14] These cultural dimensions are related to the basic problems with which all human societies must cope: individualism, power distance, uncertainty avoidance, relationship focus versus deal focus, and long-term versus short-term time orientation.[15] Included are three additional cultural variations specifically relevant to Arabic culture: time orientation, formality, and context sensitivity.[16]

Individualism versus Collectivism. Individualism refers to cultures in which people see themselves first as individuals and believe that their own interests take priority, while collectivism refers to societies in which individuals identify primarily as members of a group and believe that the group's interests take priority. Individualists are described as people who look after themselves and their immediate family only, while collectivists belong to groups, families, clans, or organizations, which look after them in exchange for loyalty.[17]

In individualist cultures, adults are expected to take care of themselves and to succeed more or less on their own. American culture provides an example of individualism. Once children grow up, they are expected to leave their parents and live on their own, and they often do not assume the responsibility of taking care of their parents. Similarly, Americans in general, and especially military leaders, tend to place great value on the contributions of the individual toward the success of an organization.

Power Distance. Power distance is a measure of human inequality in a group or organization. Power distance can be defined as "the extent to which the less powerful members of society accept and expect that power is distributed unequally."[18] High power distance suggests that the followers as well as leaders endorse the society's level of inequality.

In low-power-distance countries, individuals prefer a consultative type of leader who takes subordinates' suggestions into consideration when making a decision. In high-power-distance countries, subordinates tend to be perceived as afraid and follow their superiors' decisions without question.[19] A low-power-distance culture tends to view everyone as equal, and people tend to respect the individual. A high-power-distance culture tends to be more concerned with status and tends to accept inequality in power and authority.

Formality versus Informality. Related to the concept of power distance is the level of formality or informality in a culture. Formal cultures attach considerable importance to tradition, ceremony, social rules, and rank, while informal cultures do not. Formal cultures tend to be structured hierarchically, and individuals within the culture are very aware of their status within that hierarchy. In informal cultures, people tend to be viewed equally.

Uncertainty Avoidance. Uncertainty avoidance refers to the value an individual attaches to perceived risk—the extent to which an individual experiences uncertainty as stressful and therefore tries to avoid it. Uncertainty avoidance provides a gauge of a culture's tolerance for ambiguity and indicates the extent to which a culture encourages its members to feel either uncomfortable or comfortable in unfamiliar, unstructured situations that are novel, unknown, surprising, or different. Uncertainty-avoiding cultures try to minimize the occurrence of such situations through strict laws and rules, safety and security measures, and, on the philosophical and religious level, through a belief in absolute truth—"there can only be one Truth and we have it."[20] In contrast, uncertainty-accepting cultures are more tolerant of opinions different from the norm.

Uncertainty avoidance is closely related to the dual concepts of honor and saving face. Simply stated, saving face means that neither party in a given interaction should suffer embarrassment, which is itself often the result of uncertainty or ambiguity.

Relationship Focus versus Deal Focus. This concept refers to the importance of personal relationships in conducting business and negotiations. In relationship-focused cultures, people prefer to do business with friends, family, and persons well known to them. They always want to know their business partners very well before talking business. In these cultures, relationships are based on trust, and networking is essential for doing business. Individualist cultures tend to be deal-focused, which means they are more focused on the qualities of the deal itself rather than the person or organization offering it. Deal-focused cultures are relatively open to doing business with strangers.

In these cultures, business and personal relationships are seen as entirely separate.

Long-Term versus Short-Term Time Orientation. Long-term orientation is defined as the fostering of virtues oriented toward future rewards, especially perseverance and thrift. Short-term orientation, in contrast, seeks to foster virtues related to the past and present, especially respect for tradition, preservation of "face," and the fulfillment of social obligations.[21]

Time orientation refers to the extent members of a culture are focused on the past, present, or future in making decisions. Some cultures are very time-conscious and precise in making and keeping appointments, while others are more casual. In addition, some cultures tend to favor longer, slower deliberations, while others prefer to "get down to business."

Cognition

Cognition refers to the different processes used for problem solving, decision-making, perception, and knowledge representation of a given culture. It can be described as "the mental process of knowing, including aspects such as awareness, perception, reasoning, and judgment," and can help explain what modes of reasoning and argumentation characterize a culture, how members of a particular culture organize their thoughts about the world, and how they tend to explain behavior.[22]

A given culture can usually be characterized according to the dominant mode of reasoning used. There are three main reasoning styles:[23]

- *Dialectical reasoning.* Whether options are delineated to show their differences, or whether those options are merged to maintain possibly contradictory perspectives.
- *Hypothetical reasoning.* Whether the individual uses imagined circumstances to show implications of actions, or whether the individual grounds the analysis in context and experience.
- *Counterfactual reasoning.* Whether the individual uses counterfactual (untrue, explicitly opposite of what is known to be true) circumstances to show implications of actions.

Perception and attribution describe how people perceive objects in a scene as relating to other objects in that scene and how people of different cultures attribute causality across cultures, respectively.

Cultural Manifestations

The third component of the taxonomy of culture is cultural manifestations—specific features of a culture that display the effect of cultural influences and variations. In other words, manifestations are those behaviors, speech patterns, and attitudes that are seen on the surface. If one responds to unfamiliar or unusual cultural manifestations without understanding the cultural influences and variations that helped create them, one can have a hard time taking a strategic approach to another culture. Therefore, it is important to identify common cultural manifestations and to understand the full cultural context in which these emerged.

Using the Cultural Awareness Model to Understand Cultures

The model just described can be applied to understand key features of different cultures with which the US military may be involved. Indeed, the model can be applied across the spectrum of the strategic, operational, and tactical levels of war.

Table 1 represents a summary of the model along with the relevant definitions, which can serve to establish baselines in applying the conceptual model for cultural awareness to understanding Arab and Middle Eastern culture.

As noted earlier, cultural awareness is needed not just during war, but in the entire range of operations in which the US military can be engaged, including coordination, peacekeeping, and nation-building.

The next chapter applies this model to Middle Eastern cultures, followed by a short case study from Iraq.

Table 1. Dimensions of Cultural Variance.

Behaviors	Languages, Customs, Dress, Religion	The normal definitions for these.
The outward, observable artifacts (including structures and institutions of a culture)	Personal Space	The region around an individual, within which it is considered taboo (to varying degrees) for another individual to enter.
	Context Sensitivity	The degree to which a culture emphasizes the surrounding circumstances or context in its communications (e.g., by making extensive use of body language).
Values	Power Distance	The acceptable difference of power between a superior and a subordinate.
The base judgments of good and bad common to a culture	Uncertainty Avoidance	The value an individual attaches to a perceived risk; how much an individual experiences uncertainty as stressful, and how much he or she avoids it.
	Time Orientation	The extent to which an individual is focused on the past, present, or future in making decisions.
	Individualism	The extent to which people in a culture see themselves first as individuals and believe that their own interests take priority.
	Formality	The extent to which a culture attaches importance to tradition, ceremony, social rules, and rank.
	Relationship Focus vs. Deal Focus	The importance of personal relationships in conducting business and negotiations.
Cognition	Dialectical Reasoning	Whether options are delineated to show their differences, or whether those options are merged to maintain possibly contradictory perspectives.
The preference based strategies used in decision-making, perception, and knowledge representation	Hypothetical Reasoning	Whether the individual uses hypothetical (imagined) circumstances to show implications of actions, or grounds analysis in context and experience.
	Counterfactual Reasoning	Whether the individual uses counterfactual (untrue, explicitly opposite of what is known to be true) circumstances to show implications of actions.
	Perception	The tendency for people to perceive objects in a scene as relating to other objects in that scene.
	Attribution	How people of different cultures attribute causality across cultures.

Notes

1.   Ben Connable and Art Speyer, "Cultural Awareness for Military Operations," *Concepts and Proposals: USMC Cultural Awareness Working Group* (HWMC and MCIA, February 2005).

2.   William D. Wunderle, "Through the Lens of Cultural Awareness: Planning Requirements in Wielding the Instruments of National Power," *Warfighters: Operational Realities* (RAND Technology and Applied Sciences Group Seminar, 17 November 2004). Of course there are many uses of the term "culture" in military and social science literature. To cite just one example, *Department of Defense Dictionary of Military and Associated Terms*, Joint Publication 1-02, 12 April 2001 (as amended through 31 August 2005), defines "culture" as "A feature of the terrain that has been constructed by man. Included are such items as roads, buildings, and canals; boundary lines; and, in a broad sense, all names and legends on a map."

3.   Connable and Speyer (2005).

4.   Headquarters, Department of the Army, FM 6-0, *Mission Command: Command and Control of Army Forces* (Washington, DC: Department of the Army, August 2003), B-1 and B-2.

5.   This model was adapted from Connable and Speyer (2005) and modified to be congruent with the cognitive hierarchy found in FM 6-0, appendix B.

6.   Connable and Speyer (2005).

7.   Adapted from Carl Arthur Solberg, *Culture and Industrial Buyer Behavior: The Arab Experience* (Dijon, France, September 2002).

8.   Definition online at <http://dictionary.reference.com/search?q= cognition> (as of 2 March 2006).

9.   Benjamin Karney, Marcia Ellison, Heather Gregg, Sabrina Pagano, William Wunderle, and Scott Gerwehr, *A Framework to Analyze Cross-Cultural Diversity for Intelligence Tradecraft* (unpublished RAND research, 2006).

10.   Defense Advanced Research Projects Agency, "Urban Sunrise," Final Technical Report (Veridian/General Dynamics, February 2004), 137.

11.   Benjamin Lee Whorf, *Language, Thought and Reality* (Cambridge, MA: MIT Press, 1964).

12.   Albert Mehrabian, *Nonverbal Communication* (Chicago: Aldine-Atherton, 1972).

13.   This is adopted from Helen Altman Klein and Gary Klein, "Cultural Lens: Seeing Through the Eyes of the Adversary," presented at the 9th CGF&BR Conference, 16–18 May 2000.

14.   Geert Hofstede, "National Cultures Revisited," *Behavior Science Research*, vol. 18, 1983, 285–305.

15.   Hofstede developed these ideas based on a research project of national cultural differences across subsidiaries of a multinational corporation (IBM) in sixty-four countries. Subsequent studies by others covered students

in twenty-three countries, elites in nineteen countries, commercial airline pilots in twenty-three countries, up-market consumers in fifteen countries, and civil service managers in fourteen countries. These studies together identified and validated five independent dimensions of national culture differences.

16.   Formulations of these cultural dimensions were heavily influenced but are partially at variance with the views expressed by Geert Hofstede. Ernst Cassirer's "Circle of Humanity" also influenced my views. Cassirer's "Circle of Humanity" has six categories: Science, Language, History, Religion, Art, and Myth. Ernst Cassirer, *An Essay on Man* (New Haven, CT: Yale University Press, 1944), 68.

17.   Glen Fisher, *International Negotiation: A Cross-Cultural Perspective* (Yarmouth, ME: Intercultural Press, Inc., 1980), 130.

18.   Geert Hofstede, "A Summary of My Ideas About National Cultural Differences," online at <http://feweb.uvt.nl/center/hofstede/page3.htm> (as of 2 March 2006).

19.   Ibid.

20.   Ibid.

21.   Ibid.

22.   Karney, and others, *A Framework to Analyze Cross-Cultural Diversity for Intelligence Tradecraft.*

23.   Richard E. Nisbett and Ara Norenzayan, *Stevens' Handbook of Experimental Psychology*, 3d edition, D. L. Medin editor (New York: John Wiley & Sons, Inc., 2002).

Chapter 3

A Primer for Understanding Arabic Culture

This chapter applies the conceptual model for cultural awareness and serves as a primer for understanding key components of Arabic culture as related to the three areas of cultural awareness: cultural influences, cultural variations, and cultural manifestations. It is important to remember that these three concepts interact with each other. To achieve mission success, members of the US military need to understand these concepts and their relationship to the reactions of adversaries and allies, ways of receiving information, and decision making processes. Because of the breadth of nationalities and people included in the term "Arabic culture," this chapter also includes some examples concerning Iraq.

According to Habib Hassan Touma,[1] "The essence of Arabian culture is wrapped up in 'the Arabic language . . . Islam . . . Tradition.'" And thus "An Arab, in the modern sense of the word, is one who is a national of an Arab state, has command of the Arabic language, and possesses a fundamental knowledge of Arabian tradition, that is, of the manners, customs, and political and social systems of the culture."[2]

Because any attempt to define "Arabic culture" can be problematic, three general factors assist in determining whether to consider someone an Arab or not. First is the political factor—whether the person lives in a country that is a member of the Arab League.[3] The second is the linguistic factor—whether the person's mother tongue is Arabic. The third is the genealogical factor—whether the person can trace his or her ancestry back to the original inhabitants of the Arabian Peninsula. While different groups assess the relative importance of these factors differently, most people consider themselves Arabs because of an overlap of the above factors rather than any one factor. For example, not many people would consider themselves Arab based on the political definition without the linguistic one; thus, Kurds or Berbers usually identify themselves as non-Arab. Furthermore, Arab nationalism declares that Arabs are united in a shared history, culture, and language. Arab nationalists believe that Arab identity encompasses more than outward physical characteristics, race, or religion. A related ideology, Pan-Arabism, calls for all Arab lands to unite as one state or sovereign political entity.

Figure 4 provides a taxonomy of Arabic culture and can serve as an overview of the three main components of cultural awareness as they are relevant to Arabic culture.[4]

Cultural Influences

As discussed earlier, culture is, among other things, a shared set of traditions, belief systems, and behaviors shaped by history, religion, ethnic identity,

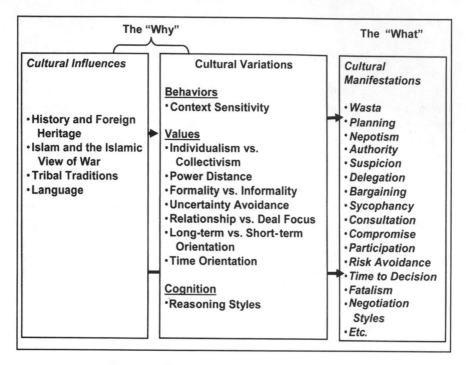

Figure 4. Taxonomy of Middle Eastern culture.

language, and nationality. The success of many postconflict operations depends on the ability of the US military to interpret and adapt to foreign cultures.[5]

While a countless number of variables influence Arabic culture, four major cultural influences will be discussed:

- Arab history and heritage.
- Islam and the role of religion.
- Tribal functions.
- Language.

Understanding these factors, however, is only the starting point for becoming culturally competent. To determine what is different about Arabic culture or any culture, US military planners must be able to understand, analyze, and then incorporate cultural influences in a way that will enable them to ask the right questions during the mission analysis process. (See chapter 4.)

History and Foreign Heritage[6]

Wars and conflicts can play a large role in a culture's self-identification. History is critical to both ethnic and national identity; most importantly, however, is not the factual history of a country or region, but the culture's dominant interpretation of that history and collective memory of the past. Because both the Ottoman Empire and later the French, Italian, and British rule influenced the cultural identity of the Arab world, the attitudes the Arabs developed under foreign rule are important to an understanding of Arabic culture.

Arab nationalists believe Arabs are united in a shared history, culture, and language. The notion of collective memory is important with regard to Arabic culture. With the formation of the Arab League in 1946, an official definition of "Arab" was put forth: "An Arab is a person whose language is Arabic, who lives in an Arabic speaking country, who is in sympathy with the aspirations of the Arabic speaking peoples."[7] Thus, one key concept within Arabic culture is the notion that such a culture truly does exist across national boundaries and regions, bringing together people of various ethnicities and origins.

The precursors of modern-day Arabs were Semitic people, originally from the Arabian Peninsula and surrounding territories, who spoke an early version of Arabic. After the adoption of Islam by Arabs (570–632), both Islam and the Arabic language spread across Northern Africa, so many North African peoples also assimilated as Arabs.[8] The modern Arab homeland stretches some 5,000 miles from the Atlantic coast of northern Africa in the west to the Sahel in the south, and covers an area of 5.25 million square miles (see figure 5).[9]

The Arab world straddles two continents, a position that has made it one of the world's most strategic regions. The Arabian Peninsula and the Gulf Region have a distinct strategic location in the southwest corner of Asia. The Arabian Peninsula is at the crossroads of Asia, Europe, and Africa. Being surrounded by important international waterways (the Hormuz Strait—the gateway to the Arabian Gulf, the Bab Al Mandab Strait, the Suez Canal, and the Red Sea), the Arabian Peninsula enjoys a strategic position in terms of communications and transportation. From an economic point of view, the Arabian Peninsula is home to the largest producers and exporters of oil, the main source of energy for the industrialized world. Currently, the Arabian Peninsula houses over 65 percent of the world's oil reserves, and Gulf countries produce 33 percent of the world's oil. Because of its communication, transport, and economic importance, as well as its strategic depth, the Arabian Peninsula, and Saudi Arabia specifically, will continue to be strategically important to the United States for the foreseeable future.[10]

While Arabs inhabit much of the Middle East and northern Africa, there are some countries in the Middle East, such as Turkey and Iran, whose populations are not predominantly Arabic. Iran is mainly a Persian culture, and most Iranians speak Farsi. Other countries, such as Egypt, Libya, and Morocco, have mixed Arab and other North African populations.

Awareness of and pride in the historic status of the Arab Empire has led some Arabs to mirror the attitudes developed in the wake of cultural dominance and to display an attitude of cultural superiority. The Arab Empire

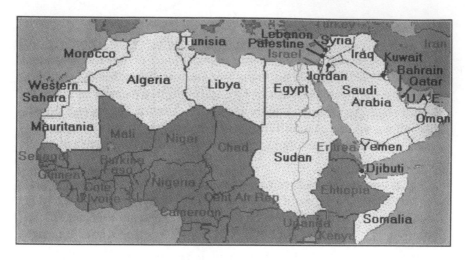

Figure 5. The Arab world.

was established during the Middle Ages and lasted more than 750 years, covering an area from the Atlantic Coast to India. Because of this, nationalistically inclined Arabs emphasize the culture's historic achievements and greatness and regard other cultures with either lenience or suspicion, depending on the culture in focus. Arabs' belief in the superiority of their own culture contrasts strongly with their economic and political dependence on Western technology.[11]

Language, ethnicity, and religion are the major components binding the Arab world together. While the most important element of what constitutes an "Arab" is culture, language is also important. Arabic is spoken throughout the Middle East and is a vital element of a shared cultural identity. Ethnicity is next, and Arabs from all Arabic lands recognize each other ethnically. In terms of national origin, Arab nationalists view Arabs as one people and advocate the establishment of one pan-Arabic state. Finally, although religion plays an important role in the Arab world, Islam is a less important factor in the cultural identity of the region than are language and ethnicity. Indeed, many Arabs remain adherents of other faiths.

The attitudes of the Arabs developed under foreign rule should also be considered. Most of the Arab-inhabited lands were a part of the Ottoman Empire until the Early Modern period. Later, French, Italian, and British rule over Arab-inhabited territories led to a greater differentiation among the Arabs. For example, "The defeat of the Arab Caliph and the ascendance of the non-Arab Ottoman Empire (1412–1918) helped institutionalize autocracy." In the Middle East during French and British rule, different parts of the former

Arab Empire were isolated from each other, leading to "clannish attitudes and inward mentality."[12]

Islam and the Role of Religion

While a number of Arab and Middle Eastern countries are tolerant of religions outside of Islam, there are some basic attitudes toward religion that the US military need to be aware of to understand the influence of religion on Arab behavior.

Although not all Arabs are religious, Islam still has an overwhelming influence over almost every aspect of everyday life in the Middle East. It is important to keep in mind that not all Arabs are religiously devout. However, as a whole, Middle Eastern societies tend to be less secular than Western societies, and even those who are not religious will experience the effects of Islam on a regular basis.

Islam is perceived as providing a common identity for people of many nations. Arabs in general do not think in terms of a combined ethnic or territorial identity, but in terms of genealogies and religion. For those of the Muslim faith in particular, religion provides a unifying force that transcends national boundaries. Bernard Lewis best articulates this attitude in his premise that "in the Western world, the basic unit of human organization is the nation . . . virtually synonymous with country. Muslims, however, tend to see not a nation subdivided into religious groups, but a religion subdivided into nations."[13] Lewis further explains that these attitudes may reflect the fact that many of the Middle East states today are relatively new entities.

Because of the central role of religion, many Arabs, particularly those of the Muslim faith, tend to believe there should be no separation of church and state in the Middle East. This is because "in the early centuries of the Muslim era, the Islamic community was one state under one ruler."[14] Muhammad (the founder of Islam) was simultaneously a prophet, a pluralistic leader and ruler, a warrior, a statesman, a teacher, and a spiritual leader. Thus, it is an unquestioned assumption that schools should teach religion and governments should promote religion. This strong reliance on religion, belief in God, and acknowledgment of God's power can manifest itself in a sense of fatalism (discussed further under "Cultural Manifestations" below), the belief that some things depend on God's will and, as a result, people cannot and should not try to control all events.[15]

Background

Because Islam plays a pervasive role in Arab countries, it can be useful to understand some of the basic tenets behind this religion.[16] Islam, the faith of the vast majority of Arabs, is not so much a religion as a form of life. It is the focal point of Arab society and provides a pattern for personal and social conduct for Muslims and non-Muslims alike, permeating their culture at every level—political, social, economic, as well as private. Most Muslims accept that the rules and norms expounded in the Quran are the result of the Prophet Muhammad's revelations and are, therefore, regarded as sacred and recognized as laws and absolute demands.

Islam arose in the early seventh century in the city of Mecca in present-day Saudi Arabia. It developed from both the Judeo-Christian tradition and the cultural values of the nomadic Bedouin tribes of Arabia. Since that time, Islam has dominated the culture of the Arab world.

Islam literally means submission to the will of God. A Muslim, therefore, is one who has submitted himself to Allah and who acknowledges Muhammad as His Prophet. Muslims consider the Prophet Muhammad to be the last in a series of prophets, which included Abraham, Moses, and Jesus, to whom God revealed His Divine Message. Islamic tradition takes into account the doctrines of Judaism and Christianity, both of which preceded it. For example, Muslims believe, as do both Jews and Christians, in one God and in an after-life. Islam also acknowledges Jews and Christians as the "people of the Book," meaning the Bible, and has granted them privileged status from the early days of the Islamic empire into modern times. This is one reason other religions have survived throughout the Arab world, even during periods of severe cultural and religious repression.

An understanding of the role of Islam in the Arab world requires an understanding of the basic tenets of the faith. The teachings of Islam are found in the holy book called the Quran, which Muslims hold to be the immutable word of God. The Quran provides Muslims with everything they need to know to lead a good and pious life. It is viewed as the unrivaled source of authority in almost all aspects of individual and group living. The Quran was revealed to Muhammad in classical Arabic.

The "hadith," the traditions and sayings of the Prophet Muhammad and his companions, complements the Quran. Together, they form the basis for the "Sunnah," or path, for devout Muslims to follow. Sunnah is the totality of the deeds, sayings, and approval of the Prophet on details of community life. The Quran and the Sunnah are the foundations of the "Sharia," or Islamic law. Both sources are indispensable. One cannot practice Islam without consulting both of them. In many Islamic countries, the Sharia provides the basis for judgment and punishment in some or all areas of life.

Islamic acts of devotion and worship are expressed in the Five Pillars of Islam. These involve not only profession of faith, but also recognition of God in all aspects of human conduct. The five pillars of Islam are summarized in table 2.

Sunni and Shiite sects. While the Islamic community throughout the world is united by the two essential beliefs in the oneness of God and the divine mission of His Prophet, there developed shortly after Muhammad's death a debate within the Islamic community over who should succeed the Prophet as leader

Table 2. The Five Pillars of Islam.

The "Shahada" or belief. The Shahada means believing and repeating that "There is no god but Allah and Muhammad is the messenger of God."
"Salat" or praying. Prayers are performed five times a day–at dawn, noon, late afternoon, sunset, and night. There is no set hour for prayers. The times for prayers vary with the movement of the sun during the seasons.
"Zakat," i.e., tithing or charity. Muslims are required to provide a portion of their personal wealth to help the less fortunate. The accepted standard is for a Muslim to provide 2.5 percent of his or her personal wealth as zakat and it is usually paid at the end of the month of Ramadan. It must be understood that giving money to the less fortunate is seen as a privilege and that there is no disgrace in receiving money through zakat.
"Sawm" or fasting. Each year, during the month of Ramadan, adult Muslims are expected to fast between dawn and sunset. Fasting includes abstaining from eating, drinking, smoking, and sexual relations.
The "Hajj" or pilgrimage. Hajj is the pilgrimage to Mecca. All Muslim are expected to make the Hajj once in a lifetime, if financially and physically able to travel.

of the faithful. This debate split the community into two major sects: Sunni and Shiite.

The Sunnis felt that the successor or caliph (from khalifa, Arabic for successor) should be chosen as other Arab leaders had been selected in the past, by consensus or election. They supported the succession of the first four caliphs, often referred to as the "rightly guided." All were companions of the Prophet Muhammad.

The Shiites believe that the succession should be through the Prophet's bloodline and that Muhammad had chosen his cousin and son-in-law, Ali, as his spiritual and secular heir. This faction is referred to as "Shia Ali" (partisans of Ali), or "Shiites." In 680 AD, Ali's son, Hussein, the Prophet's grandson, led a small rebellion against the ruling Sunni caliph. They were massacred in the battle of Karbala (located in present day Iraq).

Shia and Sunni are the two major branches of Islam and comprise 80 to 85 percent of all Muslims. The major differences between these two groups are not necessarily in beliefs and religious law, which are the same for both groups, but rather in practice and political theory. Lesser sects include the Ismailis, Alevis/Alawites, and Druze, which arose from political and doctrinal differences in the community. One mystical sect that encompasses both Sunnis and Shias is Sufiism. Sufis are individuals who believe in the need to go beyond formal religious practices and find means to commune directly with Allah. It is important to remember, however, that Muslims are in basic agreement on fundamental issues in all of these sects because they all draw on the Quran and its body of Islamic law.

The Muslim calendar is lunar and shifts in relation to the solar calendar. Just as Christians count years starting with the year of Jesus' birth, Muslims count years beginning with Muhammad's move from Mecca to Medina in

622 AD. Muslim years are labeled as A.H., Anno Hegirae, or "year of the Hijra." Major Muslim festivals include Id al-Fitr (the Fast-Breaking Festival, celebrated at the end of Ramadan) and Id al-Adha (the Festival of Sacrifice, the commemoration of Abraham's willingness to sacrifice Ishmael that takes place during the month of pilgrimage). Finally, like Christians, Muslims believe in a Day of Judgment, when righteous souls will go to heaven and wrongdoers will go to hell.

Islamic Views of War

Throughout history, religion has been an effective tool for leaders to mobilize support for political wars. Most major faiths include teachings that condemn violence and war and simultaneously promote them as morally necessary for ultimate survival. Today, religion continues to play a significant role in shaping political groups and continues to be a source of hostility between states.[17] However, different religions have varying standards for justifying war. Therefore, it is critical for current military leaders and planners to have an understanding of the potential role of Islam in justifying violent actions and the corresponding political reasons for conflict.

Islamic law sets clear guidelines as to when war is ethically right and how such wars are to be conducted. Islamic law permits war under the following three conditions: in self-defense, in defense of Islam when other nations have attacked an Islamic state, or in cases when another state is oppressing its own Muslims. The idea of unlimited conflict with no rules or boundaries is against all Islamic principles. A precept of Islam is to "Fight in the cause of God against those who fight you, but do not transgress limits. God does not love transgressors."[18]

In accordance with Islam, war is to be conducted with discipline, using a minimum of force to avoid injuring noncombatants. The Quran emphasizes that war should be fought only for noble causes without seeking any earthly reward: "Those who readily fight in the cause of God are those who forsake this world in favor of the Hereafter. Whoever fights in the cause of God, then gets killed or attains victory, we will surely grant him a great recompense."[19]

The killing of noncombatants or of prisoners of war is strictly forbidden. This is tantamount to murdering innocent lives, which leads to punishment in hell. Additionally, Muslims are forbidden to attack wounded soldiers who have ceased fighting. Muhammad, Islam's holy prophet, states in the Quran that defeated enemies should be made prisoners rather than be executed.

A good example of ideal Muslim conduct in war is the capture of Jerusalem by Saladin in 1187. Although Christians had violated a number of holy Muslim places, Saladin[20] had prohibited acts of vengeance. His army was so disciplined that there were no combat-related deaths or violence after the city surrendered. The residents were taken prisoner, but their ransom was set at a token amount.[21]

The Tribal System

Another strong cultural influence in the Arabic world comes from the tribal system. Arabic culture has strong collectivist features. Within Arab culture, the group takes precedence over the individual. Loyalty to the group is highly valued and responsibility is considered to fall on the group in its entirety rather than on any particular individual. Distant cousins, neighbors, and friends can develop bonds as strong as any bond between close family members. Because of the primacy of the group, obligations of group members to one another are wide, varied, and powerful.[22]

In this context, the tribal system gives unique advantages to a tribe's members. It is every member's duty to look after the interests of his fellow tribe, clan, or family members. All relations and loyalties in the tribal system are concentrated on the family. Tribalism has become, along with Arabism and Islam, a major ingredient of Arab and Middle East identity. Understanding the role of the tribe and the different members of the tribe is key to analyzing Arab behavior. The tribal system of Arabic cultures is shown in figure 6.

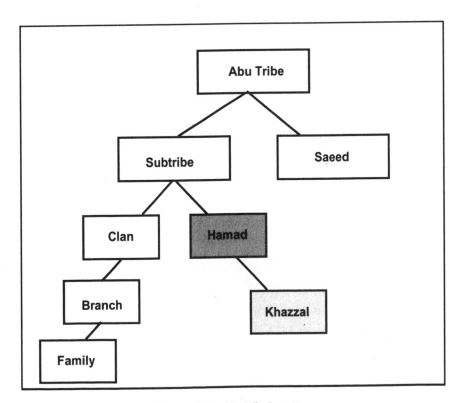

Figure 6. Arabic tribal system.

Most tribal groupings revolve around old cores and occupy the same regions in the Middle East; certain surnames reveal the area or tribe from which a family originates. Arabic names recognize five levels of a tribe. In fact, an Arab's full name can help identify the person's family, branch, clan, subtribe, and greater tribe. This system is an extension of the security net that each tribe has constructed around its members.[23] The left side of the diagram refers to the tribal level, while the right side is an example of the family name associated with the subtribe, clan, and branch, respectively.

The first level in the system is the tribe itself, which consists of several subtribes. Historically, the extended family has been the center of daily activities. The extended family, in turn, consists of clans, each with its own extended families. The subtribe is composed of a number of extended families tracing themselves back to one patrilineal father. Loyalty follows first the father's family, then the mother's family, then anyone within the greater tribe, then nationality or religion, other Arabs, and finally Westerners.

The subtribe has traditionally constituted the main unit of defense. The tribe consists of four to six subtribes, which are traced to a real or fictional ancestor. The tribe's activities are mainly political, consisting of managing relations with other tribes and governments. At this level, the tribe is led by a sheikh and advised by a council.

Furthermore, a tribe may be part of a confederation of tribes that is governed by a sheikh who, in these cases, is tremendously powerful. The power in this system is extremely centralized and is an extension of the security net that each tribe has constructed around its members. The tribe provides its members with an identity, a sense of security, and a blueprint for the resolution of conflicts, but everyday behavior is pragmatic and adaptive to specific situations.[24]

Tribal versus other forms of leadership. The understanding of both tribal and religious structures is essential because they are often in competition with other governing and administrative structures, such as town councils and local police. In a given town or village, there can be multiple forms of authority, including tribal leaders, elected councils, and prominent and educated citizens, as well as former and newly appointed leaders and religious leaders. (Figure 7 compares levels of tribal and civil authority.)

Arab culture favors centralization of authority. Superiors expect subordinates to be submissive and obedient. At the heart of the tribal system is a democratic process of consultation with elders and, in some cases, the ability of tribesmen to challenge the sheikh.

Projecting a paternal image, leaders securely occupy the top of the pyramid of authority. However, various kinds of leaders—tribal, religious, and civil—may share authority either in a complementary or competitive way. One must understand who has the power in a tribal society—formally and informally. Should a military leader go to a civil administrator, a religious cleric, a tribal leader, or the sheikh to get something done? Making the right decision

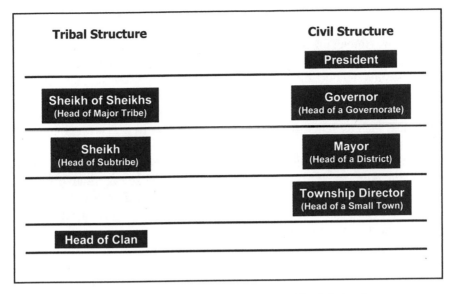

Figure 7. Arabic tribal structure compared to civil structure.

is important because if he goes to the wrong person to get something done, not only could he have empowered the wrong person, but he also might have offended any number of others in the process. The answer will be situation dependent and will vary based on the problem and the situation. Failure to recognize the different sources of authority can disrupt existing governance and resolution structures and can lead to an erosion of coalition effectiveness.

At the local level, tribal authority plays an important role. The authority of the tribal sheikhs traditionally stems from both personal influence and largess as well as from nobility of lineage.[25] Arab tribal leaders wish to maintain a higher status for themselves and their tribes based on their tribal or clan nobility, strength, reputation, or wealth. Tribal leaders, however, have limited authority within certain parameters, such as settling minor disputes. Tribal leaders tend to be masters of self-interest and survival and, therefore, may fail to represent the interests of their people. Because of this, while tribal leaders may have no positive influences on society, they are capable of significant negative influence.[26]

The religious hierarchies claim a higher status due to their relationship to Islam. The tribal system of the Shia is different from that of the Sunni in that the Shia sheikhs often had to share power with the Sadah—holy men—and the Ulema. Titles and roles vary between Sunni and Shia.

For the most part, the Sunnis adhere to the traditional tribal power structure. Sunnis have no formal clerical hierarchy and choose their leaders by consensus or appointment. Their key religious figures include Imams—primarily prayer leaders—and Qadis, who are judges of Islamic law. Unlike the Sunni, the Shia has an evolved religious hierarchy that includes Ayatollahs, Mullahs, and Ulema. Among the Shia tribes, leadership was confined to one lineage. In practice, however, nobility often turned out to be a function of the success of the leader in defending the tribal lands and managing and resolving intratribal conflicts. Contemporary tribal authority largely stems from the fact that the former regimes delegated it to them. Tribal influence is derived from personal attributes, such as generosity, honor, and the ability to deal with government officials.

Governors, mayors, and police are modestly influential within the community. Civil administrators and elected officials are looked on as civil servants and are expected to serve citizens and maintain civil functions within their area. In Iraq, because Baath Party ties largely determined their influence in the past, civil administrators and elected officials are not always highly respected.

The Arabic Language

Understanding some key points about the Arabic language is necessary to gain insight into the Arabic culture. For Arab and Middle Eastern countries, the Arabic language reinforces one's identity and is both a symbol and substance of group cohesion. It influences how a person perceives the world and expresses reality.[27] Arabic is one of four major languages used in the Middle East today, the others being Turkish, Farsi, and English, the last of which has replaced French as the primary second language of the educated elite.

The native language of 220 million people and the official language of more than twenty-one countries throughout the Arabian Peninsula and North Africa is Arabic. As the language of Islam, it affects more than one billion people in the Islamic world. In 1973, it was named the sixth official language of the United Nations and a working language in the Organization of African Unity. It is the fourth most widely spoken language in the world after Mandarin Chinese, English, and Spanish. Furthermore, Arabic has recently been reinstated as a second tongue in Iran, Pakistan, and the southern part of the Philippines. Besides Arabic, over ten languages retain the Arabic script—the most prominent being Urdu, Persian, Pashto, Kurdish, and Sindhi.[28]

Arabic has both written and spoken forms; to be literate, Arabs must be able to read and write Arabic and speak their local dialect. Modern Standard Arabic, also known as Classical Arabic, is the standard written language. This is the same across all countries and regions in which Arabic is used. Although not commonly used in daily speech, Modern Standard Arabic is used in formal discussion, speeches, and news broadcasts. Much more common in everyday speech is the use of either Formal Spoken Arabic or one of several dialects. There are five predominant dialects: Egyptian, Levantine (Syria, Lebanon), Peninsular (Saudi Arabia, Jordan, and the Gulf States), Magrebi (Morocco, Tunisia), and Iraqi. These are typically used in conversation only and are not used for written communication. Formal Spoken Arabic is a combination of Modern Standard Arabic and one of the dialects. People use it to converse with Arabs whose dialect is different from their own.[29]

Although the Arabic language can take different forms, depending on whether it is written or spoken and depending on the region, the Arabic language is a unifying force that serves to reinforce cultural identity across regions and national boundaries. Arabic is both a symbol and a substance of group cohesion. Primarily because Arabic is the language of the Quran, Arabs believe it was chosen by God and therefore is superior to other languages. Indeed, rather than adopt some other sort of religious symbol (e.g., a cross or star of David), Islam uses the written word of God in the form of calligraphy as a symbol of the religion. As such, Arabs have considerable respect for both written and spoken Arabic. In fact, "some pious people feel that anything written in Arabic should be burned when no longer needed or at least not left on the street to be walked on or used to wrap things because the name of God probably appears somewhere."[30]

Thus, according to James Coffman, a person "who studies and thinks in Arabic will develop distinct historical and cultural references, cognitive approaches, attitudes and styles of reasoning."[31] Because of this, every Arab government, regardless of its political or social character, uses the symbolic power of the Arab language in its drive toward national modernization, authentication, and uniformization. Understanding the importance of the Arabic language in the study of Middle East and Arab culture is essential to mission success.

Cultural Variations

The second set of cultural factors in the model describes cultural variations. As described in the previous chapter, these traits can be divided into three broad categories: behaviors, values, and cognition.[32] (Examples from Iraq are incorporated into the discussion where appropriate.)

Behaviors

As discussed earlier, some languages have a high degree of context sensitivity: the meaning of words can vary significantly according to context. The Arabic language tends to be highly context-sensitive; that is, the meaning of what is said must be interpreted through context rather than words alone. One can take the written word of bin Laden, give it to fifteen native Arab speakers, and get fifteen different translations. Comprehension depends on understanding what bin Laden said with respect to any historical allusions he may have referred to. In cultures with high context-sensitivity, written language can be particularly difficult to decipher because so much of the interpretation of language typically depends on aspects of the spoken context that are not available with written words alone, such as what the speaker's eyes are doing while he talks and what his body movements are.

The Arabic language ranks second only to Japanese in terms of its sensitivity to context. For example, the Arabic word "harem" can refer to the "living quarters reserved for wives and concubines and female relatives in a Muslim household."[33] This definition provides one accurate meaning of the term; however, in Arabic, the word "harem" can have several meanings based on the context of its use. It can also mean taboo, sacred, wife, prohibited, interdicted, or sanctuary.[34] Context allows one word to have many and often conflicting meanings. A man's wife is sacred to him but taboo to others. Many other words in Arabic have multiple, complex meanings that can be understood only in context. The same word in Arabic can mean push or pull or negotiate. If one person is standing in front of another, the two people can be said to be "pulling together" in dialogue, or "repelling each other"; the "correct" meaning can be determined only according to context.

Communication with speakers of Arabic requires the ability to "read" beyond what is being said in words, and to understand nonverbal communications. Space orientation differs across cultures. Attitudes toward physical space have to do with territory, divisions between private and public, comfortable personal distance, comfort or lack of comfort with physical touch and contact, and expectations about where and how contact will take place.[35] When communicating with Arabs, one must pay attention to body language, eye movements, and hand gestures. Many dimensions of nonverbal communication can contradict, emphasize, or serve as a substitute for verbal messages.

In addition, the Arabs' sense of "personal space" differs significantly from that of Americans. In the United States, people conduct face-to-face business exchanges at a distance of about five feet, which is within the so-called "social zone." In the Middle East, however, Arabs tend to stand much closer, often less than 1 foot apart. Americans tend to unconsciously back away from such close contact and in doing so risk offending their counterparts. Because social behavior is culture-dependent, competent planners must become familiar with the role-related behaviors of a particular culture. Arab men are also more likely than Americans to touch each other when talking, and it is not unusual for a man to take another man's hand when talking or to kiss or hug another man when meeting. Many Americans find these gestures unusual and feel uncomfortable if they occur. However, to work effectively with Arabs, it can be useful to become accustomed to the Arabic sense of personal space, especially to win respect.

Values

Values are principles for evaluating alternatives or consequences in decision-making and establish a basis for judgments of good and bad within a culture. As illustrated in figure 8, the values found in Arabic culture can be used to provide a lens through which to see the world as a member of that culture sees it.[36]

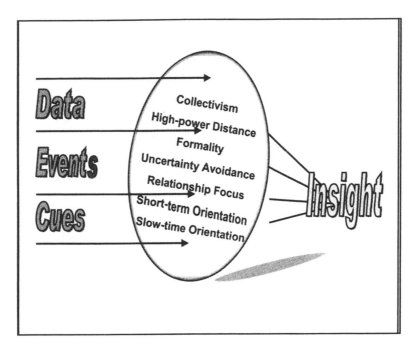

Figure 8. How values can provide a cultural lens for understanding.

Collectivism. Those in Middle Eastern cultures will go to great lengths to reach decisions through consensus, where every participating member, not just a majority, is able to agree. In collective societies, everybody belongs to a certain group. This group protects its members and expects their loyalty as return. Arab societies are collectivist. Instead of asserting their separateness and privacy as independent individuals, Arabs tend to interact as members of a group, whether family, clan, village, neighborhood, tribe, etc. Group norms guide individual behavior and, in general, Arabs display a high need for social approval. Originality and independence of judgment are not valued as highly as teamwork. As the Arabic saying goes, "A nail standing out will be hammered down." Shaming is the primary instrument through which Arab society enforces conformity. The group often determines a person's identity, status, and prospects for success in life. As a result, Arabs are subjected to immense family and community pressures, and they will often sacrifice a few individuals for the good of the many. The influence of collectivism in the Middle East can help to explain why so many are willing to sacrifice their lives for the good of the "in-group."

High-power distance. As described in the previous chapter, power distance can be defined as "the extent to which the less powerful members of society accept and expect that power is distributed unequally."[37] In a high-power distance culture, people are more concerned with status and tend to accept inequality in power and authority. Arabic society tends to be a very high-power distance culture. A common Arabic saying reflects this: "The eye cannot rise above the eyebrow," meaning the eye cannot change its position in life. Because Arabs tend to accept inequality as a fact, those on the bottom of the hierarchy may not show a lot of movement or initiative to change their lot. This, in turn, can inhibit out-of-the-box thinking and individual initiative.

Formality. The business culture found in most of the Arab world is formal. Middle Eastern cultures do not equate formality with coldness, and Arabs typically value respect and take a more formal approach than do Americans to business dealings and negotiations. Respect in business is important even when dealing with an adversary. Arab hospitality dictates that when an adversary is invited into one's home, the host is responsible for his safety. Failing to provide adequate hospitality will result in a loss of face.

Arabs are title and rank conscious and they know US Army hierarchy and rank structure. It is important, therefore, for US military personnel working in the Middle East to call their counterparts by title and family names unless specifically asked to do otherwise. Americans should try to convey an attitude of propriety and decorum through both verbal and nonverbal clues. Formality appears to be related to power distance. Formal cultures tend to have high-power distance in their organizations, while informal cultures are more likely to be low-power distance countries.

Uncertainty avoidance. Arabic people typically try to avoid uncertainty and risk in their daily activities. Uncertainty-avoiding cultures try to minimize the possibility of risk through strict laws and rules, safety and security measures, and, on the philosophical and religions level, through a belief in absolute truth. In such cultures, the concepts of honor and "saving face" can be very important. These concepts can make it difficult for Arabs to say "no" to a request because to do so would be impolite. Thus, they are reluctant to offend others—even if they intentionally mislead them. Thus, a "yes" to an Arab might mean, "Yes, I understand you," rather than "yes, I agree." Because of this, it is essential to be able to read between the lines because what is left unsaid or unwritten may be just as important as what is said or written.

Relationship focus. The Arab world is a strong relationship-focused culture—the relationship is what is important. Relationship-focused people prefer to do business with friends, families, and persons well known to them. For Arabs, business is personal. In a relationship-focused culture, it is important to understand the patterns for building relationships and to take time to establish trust and friendship. Understanding this is essential to mission success in the Middle East. To get things done for the long term, US military leaders and other personnel must spend time gaining credibility and building relationships.[38] A foreigner cannot expect to go in, say these things need to happen tomorrow, and then be surprised when all does not go well. Focusing on relationships means taking time to have tea, talk about the weather, discuss families and the latest soccer scores, and build a relationship. US rotation policies can be problematic because they make relationship building more difficult. When dealing with Arabs, one must go slow to achieve lasting success.

Short-term orientation. Arabs tend to have what can be called a short-term orientation, meaning they tend to foster virtues oriented toward future rewards, particularly perseverance and thrift. As noted earlier, the concept of honor and the preservation of face is an exceptionally strong element in Middle Eastern cultures. When an Arab feels that something is threatening his personal dignity, he may be obliged to deny it, even in the face of facts to the contrary. Arabs will rarely admit to errors if doing so will cause them to lose face. "To Arabs, honor is more important than facts."[39] An Arabic saying epitomizes this ideal: "Honor cannot be returned from harm until blood is spilled." The saying means that revenge is a necessary and value-sustained cultural difference that sanctions and even honors the idea of an "eye for an eye."[40] The military must understand this when dealing with Arab counterparts.

Slow-time orientation. In the Middle East, time orientation, also called polycronic orientation, tends to appear slow by American standards. In slow-time cultures, multiple tasks are handled at the same time, and time is subordinate to interpersonal relations.[41] As discussed earlier, the Arabic language is past-oriented—the perfect verb form is past tense masculine, and provides little linguistic structure for talking about the future, which "is not man's concern but that of the Divine."[42] For example, Americans are very time conscious and very precise about appointments, while Arab cultures tend to be more casual about time. If an Arab host arranges a meeting at three o'clock, he most likely means "Inshallah" (Arabic for "If God wills, as God pleases"); in other words, the appointment is not precise.

Cognition

The third form of cultural variation is cognition: preference-based strategies used in the decision-making, perception, and knowledge representation of a given culture. Arabic processes of cognition mean that Middle East concepts of reality and truth may be different from their US counterparts. What individuals are willing to accept as a normal part of reality is a complex result of personality, beliefs, cultural environment, and life history. Perception of reality will influence social cohesion, industriousness, views of conflict and forgiveness, charity toward others, attachment to material comforts, capacity for suffering, and willingness to die for a cause. Truth, on the other hand, is tied to subjective experience, sources of knowledge, and local interpretation. It is an objective fact rather than an independent variable. Even though foreign counterparts may come to the same conclusions as Americans do, they may use a different process to reach that conclusion. One must understand how Middle East cultures make decisions—how they come to conclusions.[43]

Cultural Manifestations

The third part of the cultural awareness model is manifestations: the ways in which cultural influences and variations are visible in a culture. Table 3 provides an overview of some key cultural manifestations seen in Arabic culture. A brief explanation is provided for each item. Since most of these

Table 3. Prominent Cultural Manifestations in Arabic Culture.

Manifestation	Brief Explanation
Wasta	Wasta encompasses anything from networking and lobbying to nepotism, bribing, and corruption. There are two forms of wasta: mediation and intercession (to achieve a benefit).
Planning	Research on Arab management practices asserts that planning—although seen as an important element by managers—receives only scant resources and time. Managers instead spend their time assigning work duties to their subordinates and supervising and monitoring their performance.*
Nepotism	Favoritism is typically granted to relatives or close friends without regard to their merit. Nepotism usually takes the form of employing relatives or appointing them to high office.
Deference to authority	Arab culture favors centralization of authority. Subordinates are expected to be submissive and obedient to their superiors.
Suspicion	Arabs, in general, are very "conspiracy-theory oriented." A conspiracy theory defies an official or dominant understanding of events under the claim that those events are not natural occurrences, but the result of manipulations by two or more individuals or various secretive powers.
Tendency to delegate	The role of leaders is to spend their time assigning work duties to their subordinates and supervising and monitoring their performance.*
Sycophancy	There can be a tendency for some subordinates to behave with servile flattery or the fawning behavior of a sycophant.
Consultation	At the heart of the tribal system is a fairly democratic process of consultation with the tribal elders and sheikhs.
Tendency to seek compromise	Those in Middle Eastern cultures will go to great lengths to reach decisions through consensus, wherein every participating member, not just a majority, is able to agree.
Participation	At the heart of the tribal system is a fairly democratic process of consultation with elders and, in some cases, the ability of tribesmen to challenge the sheikh.
Risk avoidance	Risk avoidance deals with a society's tolerance for uncertainty and ambiguity. Arabs tend to feel threatened by uncertainty and ambiguity, and thus try to avoid these situations.
Fatalism	A prominent philosophical doctrine in the Middle East holds that all events are predetermined in advance for all time and that human beings are powerless to change them.
Negotiation style	Negotiation style helps display a culture's thought and behavior, its willingness to take compromise and embrace risk.

*H.S. Atiyyah, "Research Note: Research in Arab Countries" (published in Arabic). See also Carl Arthur Solberg, *Culture and Industrial Buyer Behavior: The Arab Experience* (Dijon, France, September 2002).

manifestations are familiar, this chapter includes a detailed discussion only of two of the more unfamiliar and complicated concepts: wasta and fatalism. (Appendix C addresses Middle East negotiation styles.)

Wasta. Many activities in Arabic culture depend on wasta, i.e., a mediator or connection. Simply put, wasta refers to third parties who can influence the outcome of events. Wasta can mean personal influence, networking, prestige and political power, and influence peddling all rolled into one. Wasta has a central face-saving function that is important in collectivist, honor-based, tribal societies. Historically, wasta was associated with conflict resolution. Today, however, its main goal has changed from defusing tribal conflict to acquiring economic benefits. Patrons who once helped their followers for prestige now seek monetary rewards. In many places in the Middle East, it is conventional wisdom to use local intermediaries "to expedite the processing of official documents, for such a person understands what is needed beyond technical requirements of the law: the function of gifts, flattery, and reciprocal favors to move things through the bureaucratic mill."[44] While wasta is considered a form of "humanizing bureaucracy," it makes life miserable for conscientious officials trying to live by the law who are called on to break the law to help a family or tribal member. Understanding wasta is critical to decision-making in the Middle East, "for wasta pervades the culture of all Arab countries and is a force in every significant decision. Wasta is a way of life."[45]

Fatalism. Arabic culture tends toward fatalism, the belief that people are powerless to control events. Fatalism is the belief that God has "direct and ultimate control of all that happens. If something goes wrong, people can absolve themselves of blame or can justify doing nothing to make improvements or changes by assigning the cause to God's will."[46] Significant events of the past still bring strong emotions and are very relevant in Arabic society. Because of this, anything that will happen beyond now is in God's hands. Fatalism can influence many aspects of Middle Eastern life, including whether or not to keep appointments. As noted earlier, for most Arabs, setting a specific time to meet does not necessarily constitute an appointment and no disrespect is meant if they fail to keep that appointment. While the concept of fatalism is more prevalent among more traditional Arabs than the educated elite, foreigners, who are very likely to encounter Arab fatalism in some form or another, still should understand this concept.

As the US leaders and soldiers consider how to win the hearts and minds of the people in the Arab Middle East, they can gain some useful insights by comparing aspects of US and Arabic culture. (Table 4 summarizes some of the key differences between Arab and US culture.) As military leaders begin the process of planning military operations, they ought to think first about their own purposes and culture and then undertake a more intensive and holistic analysis of the culture or set of cultures to be addressed. In doing this, it is important for Americans to understand where US culture sits on the cultural

Table 4. The Cultural Gap Between the Middle East and the United States.

Value	Higher	Lower
Power Distance: Cultures in which decisions are made by the boss simply because he or she is the boss.	Middle East	United States
Individualism: Cultures in which people see themselves first as individuals and believe that their own interests take priority.	United States	Middle East
Relationship Focus vs Deal Focus: Refers to the importance of personal relationships in conducting business and negotiations.	Middle East	United States
Uncertainty Avoidance: Cultures in which people want predictable and certain futures.	Middle East	United States
Long-Term Orientation: Cultures that maintain a long-term perspective.	United States	Middle East
Time Orientation: Cultures that perceive time as a scarce resource and that tend to be impatient.	United States	Middle East
Formality: Cultures that attach considerable importance to tradition, ceremony, social rules, and rank.	Middle East	United States
Context Sensitivity: Cultures that emphasize the surrounding circumstances (or context), make extensive use of body language, and take the time to build relationships and establish trust.	Middle East	United States

continuum. Following is a case study on Iraq. The framework focuses on overall group patterns of perception and reasoning versus trying to predict individual actions and behaviors.

Case Study: Iraq

This subsection contains a discussion of prominent cultural factors relevant to US military operations in Iraq. (For a discussion of the role of culture in US operations in Somalia, please see appendix D.)

For the most part, Iraqis are Arab, and, as such, have many if not all of the same influences and values outlined throughout this chapter. This section highlights some Arabic cultural influences that have been particularly prominent in Iraq. Iraqi heritage, religion, and tribal structure in particular have been key cultural influences. Iraqis tend to think of themselves as survivors. They have endured decades of brutal dictatorship and survived years of international sanctions compounded by a poor economy. To survive has sometimes meant a reliance on and acceptance of smuggling, crime, and corruption—subversive social traits that were encouraged by Saddam Hussein.[47]

Iraqis also have little sense that they are part of a cohesive society. At the conclusion of major combat operations (MCO) in Iraq, Iraqi civil structure was in disarray. Those who had government jobs were now unemployed. Because no one paid taxes, there was no investment in the community. The police were focused on survival of the regime; therefore, law enforcement was weak or, in many cases, nonexistent. Because of this, there was little or no trust in the government, and society defaulted to a collective tribal system.[48]

Heritage. Understanding the context of the military theater of operations requires comprehension of some fundamentals about Iraq's history and geography. The following is a brief synopsis of Iraq's history.[49]

History. Iraq covers 437,072 square kilometers and has a population of 24.7 million, 40 percent of whom are younger than fourteen years old. Being the cradle of civilization means its history dates back well before 2500 BC. Iraq was part of the Ottoman Empire until 1914, when World War I broke out and the empire aligned with Germany and lost. When the Alliance, led by Great Britain, won the war and it had more than one million men in the Arab Middle East. Great Britain drew a new map of Iraq that was not based on naturally occurring and longstanding cultural groupings, but on what would be best for its interests in Iraqi oil. The British wanted to create a system that would protect Western oil companies in the Middle East.

Today, Iraq is composed of three provinces separated by both natural and physical boundaries and historically distinct cultures tied to three dominant religious identities: Mosul in the north (Kurds), Baghdad in the center (Sunnis), and Basra in the south (Shiites). The Shiites believe a direct blood descendant of Muhammad should lead Muslims, whereas the Sunnis do not. The country is also home to many tribal chiefs: Jews, Christians, and Azeris who contribute to a very diverse and fractious population, all seeking to rise to the top and take control of the country.

Iraq's Baath Party was founded in Syria by two teachers educated in France and began as a force to combat British and French domination in Iraq and to foster Arab unity and freedom. The party came to power in Iraq in 1968 and retained power until its demise in April 2003. The party adopted a mild form of socialism. Under Saddam Hussein, the party embarked on a program to eradicate illiteracy; built hospitals, schools, and universities; and played an important role in liberating women and establishing a secular government. At the same time, Saddam ruled ruthlessly and practiced strict authoritarian control to keep the country together and to cement and protect his power.

As a state, Iraq is still relatively young, but it does not have a single cultural identity. It was founded through political and diplomatic maneuvering and held together by an authoritarian and secular government. Throughout its history, Iraq has been a battleground among tribal, ethnic, religious, and national forces, and it remains a hotbed of social tensions. In the Muslim world, Iraq has been the center of conflict between the Sunnis in Turkey and the Shiites in Iran.[50] Today the Kurds, Sunnis, and Shiites continue to vie for power.

Attitudes toward foreigners. Iraq's history, as well as the history of Islam itself, has caused the people to view foreigners, particularly Westerners, with a certain level of distrust. Given that Iraq's history has been fraught with invasion and control by outsiders, one could predict with relative certainty that outsiders would not be trusted. A common sentiment among Iraqis is that the United States went into Iraq for its own economic interests and not for the greater welfare of the Iraqi people.

This distrust colors the meaning and implications of nearly every event that occurs in the region—especially events that surround US policy and military actions. The average Iraqi does not understand why the same military that expelled Iraq from Kuwait in a hundred-hour war in Operation Desert Storm, destroyed the Taliban, and overthrew Saddam Hussein, cannot provide security or restore electrical power. Many people suspect the United States of intentionally keeping the power off.

To understand Iraqis' views of the United States, one must look at it through their eyes. What is the history of invasion and occupation in Iraq? Since the Middle Ages, the Muslims, Greeks, Mongols, Ottomans, British, and Iranians have invaded Iraq. No matter whether US operations in Iraq are officially labeled liberation or occupation, the average Iraqi considers Americans to be occupiers. The Iraqis' shared history, experiences, and myths will influence their perspectives of what will happen next, despite their being told anything different.

Furthermore, Iraqis are still not certain what the future holds for them. Many Iraqis, especially those in the south, are wary of trusting the United States. Again, one need only look at the past to see why. In late February 1991, when the Iraqi Army was retreating from Kuwait, the first President Bush encouraged Iraqis to rise up against Saddam, implying that America would back a rebellion. American support did not materialize and the intifada was viciously suppressed.[51] Today the United States is asking the Iraqi people to expose themselves and rise up again to assist the Coalition in defeating the insurgency. However, they remain afraid and are uncertain of what the outcome will be. A lack of trust remains.

Tribal and family influences. Iraqis place trust in family, tribal, and village ties. Outsiders are distrusted and their motivations suspect. Given the in-group nature of Iraq's culture, as well as Iraq's porous borders and history of invasion, it would be predictable that small cells of terrorists or extremists might go undetected or ignored because the Iraqi people are focused on their own in-groups that tend to keep to themselves.

Tribalism has become, along with Arabism and Islam, a major ingredient of Iraqi identity. Tribes also play something of a unifying role in contemporary Iraq. Many encompass Sunni and Shia sections. Even Saddam Hussein's Al-bu Nasir tribe has a Shia branch in the Najaf area. Tribal loyalty among Iraqi Arabs is far from complete, but when combined with repression and social and economic benefits, Saddam Hussein's tribal policy created a strong bond among the Arab tribes and the regime.[52]

In the past, Sunni Arabs, as the ruling elite, have tried to balance and reconcile Iraqi nationalism and a broader pan-Arabism. However, a pan-Arab ideology, by its very nature, precludes a separate Shia identity and excludes the Kurds. A divide-and-rule strategy accompanied these efforts, which discouraged contacts between the Shia and the Kurds. The geographic location of the Sunnis in the center of the country facilitated this approach. In addition to benefiting from the former political hierarchy in Iraq, Sunni Arabs tended to support the Baathist regime, if only because it represented a bulwark against possible Shia or Kurdish power.[53]

In Iraq, the tribal system in most of the Shia Arab south is different from that of the Sunni Arab center-north because the Shia sheikhs often had to share power with the sadah—holy men—and the ulema. Those Shia clerics a strong source of leadership, were systematically assassinated or executed by Saddam's regime. As a result, the Shia religious establishment was greatly weakened.[54] While there remains a strong Iranian influence today, most Shias remain independent.

Tribes in Iraq are a reality and should be dealt with from a position of understanding their roles and power. Failure to do so can result in their gaining disproportionate power to the exclusion of educated Iraqis and those not affiliated with the more powerful tribes. Because of the Iraqis' experiences with the Baathist regime's totalitarianism in the past, there will always be some tension between tribal traditions and the civil administrators and elected officials. In later years, the regime grafted tribal traditions, such as blood money and honor killings, onto the legal system, and respected tribal customs when prosecuting criminal cases. Americans' failure to understand the role of tribalism in Iraq has led some units to empower certain tribal structures disproportionately, while virtually ignoring others.[55]

Religion. We have already discussed the importance of religion in the Middle East. In Iraq, it is necessary not only to understand Islam, but the unique versions of Islam that exist in the different areas of Iraq and the role that each plays.[56] Muslim religious holidays can have practical implications for US operations in Iraq. Coalition forces face a number of such holidays. The Hajj and Ashura are particularly noteworthy not only because of their religious significance, but also because they involve the cross-border movements of thousands of people. For instance, in 2003, forces throughout Iraq had to deal with roughly 70,000 pilgrims going to Saudi Arabia for the Hajj. The majority of the pilgrims took an overland route through the Western Desert (Anbar province), drove into Saudi Arabia, and were transported by air from Kuwait City. This involved gaining country clearance into Kuwait and obtaining visas from Saudi Arabia. The pilgrimage affected tactical-level maneuver, and Civil Affairs (CA) units were faced with the need to establish a temporary camp in Safwan for 32,000 pilgrims who were awaiting Saudi visas. The actions of

CA forces involved erecting tents, providing food and water, and coordinating directly with the Red Crescent.

Ashura is a Shia religious holiday that involves the movement of tens of thousands of Shias from Iran and Iraq to Najaf and Karbala (central Iraq). Like the Hajj, Ashura is an annual event that is considered a religious requirement. The prevention of pilgrims from fulfilling either the rituals of the Hajj or Ashura will have negative national and international consequences. Consequently, it is critical that CA forces be properly educated to advise commanders on the importance of providing security, support, and passage to Muslims for pilgrimages. It is noteworthy to mention that this is not limited to Iraq. Coalition forces operating in Afghanistan have similarly had to take measures to facilitate the movement of pilgrims to the Hajj.[57]

Self-identification. Instead of asserting their separateness and privacy as independent individuals, Iraqi Arabs tend to interact as members of a group—family, clan, village, neighborhood, tribe, etc. Group norms guide individual behavior and Iraqi Arabs display a high need for social approval. Shaming is the primary instrument with which Iraqi Arab society enforces conformity. The group often determines a person's identity, status, and prospects for success in life. As a result, Iraqi Arabs are subjected to immense family and community pressures.[58]

An Arab identifies first with his family, and then his extended family, his village, and his tribe, followed by his country and his religious sect. Religious identification may vary from very weak to very strong, based on an individual's personal views of religion. Look at the names Arabs use . . . bin Laden means "son of Laden." Abu Nidal means "father of Nidal." Thus, even Arabic names reflect their strong family and tribal ties. This is not to say there are no problems. There are intra- and intertribal conflicts. Like any other society, they vie for power and there are many subsects and clans all with their own agendas. There are natural tensions and problems that occur in groups like these. They pick their tribal leaders by consensus, and the tribal leaders lead by consensus. That is democracy at the grass-roots level. Once a tribal leader is in power, he is the ruler and, when he dies or moves out, they pick someone else to represent them. Iraqis, in fact, understand basic democratic concepts at the lower levels.

Power distance. Iraq is a relatively high-power distance country where authority is accepted and people wait for those in authority to act on their behalf: In general, the Iraqi people mistrust outsiders and will wait to see what their leaders think and will look to them for direction. This means that communications from outsiders are more effective if targeted messages are directed at the multiple leaders who battle amongst themselves for power.

Grass-roots organizing is not the norm in Iraq. Therefore, it could have been predicted that the Iraqis would not be quick to self-organize following the toppling of Saddam Hussein. Many Iraqis look to strong religious leaders to provide authority and direction. They try to find one who can lead them and will rally around this leader, looking to the strength of the leader to pull them through tough times and into a position of group dominance. The murder or death of a religious leader will typically provoke strong negative reaction among this population and could be expected to cause a backlash.

Because of the important role played by leaders, direct appeals to the Iraqi people are typically of limited success. As a result, the marginal effectiveness of US propaganda appealing directly to the people with flyers and radio broadcasts should not have come as a surprise. Indeed, as US military leaders formulate themes and messages for an Arabic population, they must realize that if the people are not inclined to take the initiative to change things—even for the better—then military-influenced operations might not have much impact on the common people.

Counterfactual thinking. In Iraq, the pattern of thinking is based on the analysis of past events through the eye of experience. Given that Iraq's history has been fraught with invasion and control by outsiders, one could expect certainty that outsiders would not be trusted. Iraq is a country renowned as the cradle of civilization, yet is now beholden to outsiders for the basic necessities of life and the competence needed to manage in the modern world.[59] How is this collective past experience remembered and institutionalized among the people? A common sentiment among Iraqis is that the United States went into Iraq for its own economic interests and not for the greater welfare of the Iraqi people. Therefore, it is especially important for US soldiers to maintain a positive image if the United States hopes to gain the acceptance of the people, particularly because of the major role played by honor and shame in Iraqi culture.

Fatalism and collectivism. Iraq's religious history has led to a pattern of belief rooted in fatalism. There is a general acceptance of circumstances, a belief that people have little control over what happens to them and they must accept the fate handed to them by God. Islamic fatalism means an acceptance of death. Fatalism leads to a tendency to accept circumstances and wait for them to change rather than try to control them actively. Iraq is also a collectivist, or group-oriented, culture. Fatalism combined with collectivism could lead to a willingness to sacrifice individual life for the good of the in-group. It is likely the US forces on the ground have a difficult time understanding why Iraqis might passively accept their circumstances rather than take matters into their own hands. Muslims believe in fate, but how much they do to change that fate can be used to get them to help themselves. There is an old Arabic saying, *"Tie your camel and leave the rest up to God."* The United States has to convince them that we need them to do their part by "tying the camel."

Competition. There is inherent competition among different subgroups in Iraq originating in religious and historical roots and natural geographic boundaries. Competition for resources and power is likely to continue and intensify when there is a power void.

Conclusion

Success on the battlefield results from the ability of leaders to understand the human terrain and think and adapt faster than the enemy, and from the ability of soldiers to make their way successfully in an environment of uncertainty, ambiguity, and unfamiliarity. Cultural awareness is the ability to recognize and understand the effects of culture on people's values and behaviors, and implies an understanding of the need to consider cultural terrain in military operations, a knowledge of which cultural factors are important for a given situation and why, and a specified level of understanding for a target culture.

As such, this chapter demonstrates a methodology for understanding key components of Arabic culture as related to the three areas of cultural awareness: cultural influences, cultural variations, and cultural manifestations. It also provides a way for American soldiers and leaders to understand how cultural awareness can be used to influence military operations. In addition, this chapter shows how the conceptual model for cultural awareness could be adapted to the Middle East and applied it specifically to Iraq. (Appendix C uses the model to understand Middle East negotiation styles and assist in preparing soldiers to conduct negotiations in the Middle East. Appendix D uses the model to shed light on the implications of culture for US operations in Somalia.)

The next chapter considers ways to incorporate the cultural awareness model in US military training and doctrine.

Notes

1.   Habib Hassan Touma was a composer and musicologist who compiled a number of authoritative books on Arab music in his lifetime. Dr. Touma died in 1998.

2.   Habib Hassan Touma, *The Music of the Arabs*, new expanded edition, trans. Laurie Schwartz (Portland, OR: Amadeus Press, 1996), xviii.

3.   Arab League is the informal name of the League of Arab States, a voluntary association of independent countries whose peoples are mainly Arabic speaking. Its stated purposes are to strengthen ties among the member states, coordinate their policies, and promote their common interests. The Arab League was founded in Cairo in 1945 by Egypt, Iraq, Lebanon, Saudi Arabia, Syria, Transjordan (Jordan as of 1950), and Yemen. Member countries include Algeria, Bahrain, Comoros, Djibouti, Egypt, Iraq, Jordan, Kuwait, Lebanon, Libya, Mauritania, Morocco, Oman, Palestine, Qatar, Saudi Arabia, Somalia, Sudan, Syria, Tunisia, United Arab Emirates, and Yemen. Other countries of interest include Armenia, Bosnia, Chechenya, Eritrea, Iran, Israel, Kurdistan, Turkey, and Western Sahara. See also www.arableagueonline.org.

4.   Adapted from Carl Arthur Solberg, *Culture and the Industrial Buyer Behavior: The Arab Experience* (Dijon, France, September 2002).

5.   See Appendix B, "The 27 Articles of T. E. Lawrence."

6.   For a more in-depth overview of the Arabic people and the Middle East, see Bernard Lewis, *The Middle East: A Brief History of the Last 2,000 Years* (New York: Scribner, 1995).

7.   Dictionary.LaborLawTalk.com, search word "Arab," online at <http://encyclopedia.laborlawtalk.com/Arab> (as of 23 August 2005).

8.   The foundation of Islam by the Prophet Muhammad and the Islamization of Arabia during his lifetime marked the beginning of the large-scale Arab expansion outside the Arabian Peninsula and the Syrian Desert. See Raphael Patai, *The Arab Mind* (Catherleigh Press, May 2002), 13.

9.   Middle East News & World Report, Introduction to the Arab World, online at <http://www.middleeastnews.com/intoarab101.html> (as of 29 March 2005).

10.   Silas R. Johnson, Jr., "United States Military Training Mission: A Paradigm for Regional Security," *The DISAM Journal*, Summer 2001. For an overview of US strategic interests in the Middle East as well as a discussion of US plans for increasing stability in the region, see Office of the Assistant Secretary of Defense, *United States Security Strategy for the Middle East* (Washington, DC: Department of Defense, Office of International Security Affairs, May 1995). See also Anthony H. Cordesman, *US Strategic Interests in the Middle East and the Process of Regional Change* (Washington, DC: Center for Strategic and International Studies, 1 August 1996).

11.   M.M. Ahmed, *International Marketing and Purchasing of Projects: Interactions and Paradoxes—A Study of Finnish Project Exports to the Arab Countries* (Helsingfors: Swedish School of Economics and Business Administration, 1993). See also Middle East News & World Report, Introduction to the Arab World.

12.   P. Hitti, *The Arabs: A Short History* (Washington, DC: Regnery Gateway, 1985).

13.   Bernard Lewis, *The Crisis of Islam, Holy War and Unholy Terror*, Modern Library Edition (New York: Random House, Inc., 2003), xx–xxi.

14.   Ibid., xxi.

15.   Margaret K. (Omar) Mydell, *Understanding Arabs: A Guide for Westerners*, 3d edition (Yarmouth, ME: Intercultural Press, Inc., 2002), 25.

16.   This section was influenced by LTC Russell B. Crumrine, "The Middle East and North Africa: A Cultural Guide for Security Assistance Personnel," The Defense Institute of Security Assistance Management (DISAM), June 2000, 4–8. For a more definitive analysis of the role of Islam in Middle East and Arabic society, see Lewis (2003).

17.   Calvin F. Swari, Jr., *The Operational Planning Factors of Culture and Religion* (Newport, RI: US Naval War College, 13 May 2003), 3.

18.   Quran 2:190.

19.   Quran 4:74.

20.   Salah al-Din Yusuf (Saladin) was a great Muslim leader who united and led the Muslim world. In 1187, he recaptured Jerusalem for the Muslims after defeating the King of Jerusalem at the Battle of Hattin near the Lake of Galilee. When his soldiers entered the city of Jerusalem, they were not allowed to kill civilians, rob people, or damage the city.

21.   BBC, Islam, Religion & Ethics, online at <www.bbc.co.uk/religion/ethics/war> (as of 27 April 2004).

22.   John Pike, "Societal Framework," GlobalSecurity.org 2000–2005, online at <http://www.globalsecurity.org/military/world/iraq/society.htm> (as of 4 April 2005).

23.   For a more in-depth analysis of the tribal system, specifically in Iraq, see William S. McCallister, "The Iraq Insurgency: Anatomy of a Tribal Rebellion," online at <http://www.firstmonday.org/issues/issue10_3/mac/> (as of 21 March 2004).

24.   Pike, "Societal Framework."

25.   Ibid.

26.   Ben Connable and Art Speyer, "Cultural Awareness for Military Operations," *Concepts and Proposals: USMC Cultural Awareness Working Group* (HQMC and MCIA, February 2005).

27.   James Coffman, "Does the Arabic Language Encourage Radical Islam?" *Middle East Quarterly*, December 1995, online at <http://www.meforum.org/pf.php?id=276> (as of 23 February 2006).

28.   Habeeb Salloum, "The Odyssey of the Arabic Language and its Script," online at <http://www.alhewar.com/habeeb_salloum_arabic_language.htm> (as of 19 February 2005).

29.   Nydell (2002), 117.

30.   Ibid.

31.   Coffman (1995).

32.   Defense Advanced Research Projects Agency, "Urban Sunrise," Final Technical Report (Veridian/General Dynamics, February 2004), 137.

33.   WordReference.com English Dictionary, search term "harem," online at <http://www.wordreference.com/definition/harem> (as of 2 March 2006).

34.   Hans Wehr, *A Dictionary of Modern Arabic*, J. M. Cowan, editor, 4th edition (Ithaca, NY: Spoken Language Services, 1994), 201.

35.   Michelle LeBaron, "Culture-Based Negotiation Styles," July 2003, online at <http://www.beyondintractability.org/essay/culture_negotiation/> (as of 2 March 2006).

36.   Figure 8 is adapted from Helen Altman Klein and Gary Klein, "Cultural Lens: Seeing Through the Eyes of the Adversary," presented at the 9th CGF&BR Conference, 16–18 May 2000.

37.   Geert Holstede, "A Summary of My Ideas About National Cultural Differences," online at <http://feweb.uvt.nl/center/hofstede/page3.htm> (as of 23 February 2006).

38.   For example, the author was stationed in Saudi Arabia for two years. It took him six months of his first year there just to understand his role, the environment, and to learn his way around. It took him the next six months to establish solid relationships with his Saudi counterparts. It was only during the author's second year that things really began to happen. Because of the established relationships with his counterparts at the Ministry of Defense and Aviation (MODA), he was able to plan and execute an unprecedented, joint Saudi-US airborne operation [see Matthew J. Yandura, "Allies Train, Jump Together," *Soldiers Magazine*, October 2002, 43; online at <http://www4.army.mil/soldiers/archive/oct2002/pdfs/postmarks.pdf> (as of 2 March 2006)]. If the author had only been there a year, this could not have happened.

39.   Nydell (2002), 45.

40.   Glen Fisher, *International Negotiation: A Cross-Cultural Perspective* (Yarmouth, ME: Intercultural Press, Inc., 1980), 177.

41.   The concept of polycronic and monochronic cultures was introduced by E. T. Hall in *The Dance of Life: The Other Dimension of Time* (New York: Anchor Press, 1989).

42.   Fisher (1980), 130.

43.   See Patai (2002).

44.   Fisher (1980), 103.

45.   Robert B. Cunningham and Yasin K. Sarayrah, *Wasta: The Hidden*

Force in Middle Eastern Society (Westport, CT: Praeger, 1993).

46.   Nydell (2002), 44.

47.   Connable and Speyer (2005).

48.   Ibid.

49.   Much of this section was adapted from Defense Advanced Research Project Agency (2004), 126–127.

50.   For a detailed analysis of the history of Iraq from the Middle Ages to the twenty-first century, see Helen Chapin Metz, "Iraq: Historical Setting," Library of Congress Country Study, May 1988.

51.   Intifada is an Arabic word for shaking, uprising, or insurrection. This word usually refers to the Arabic resistance to Israeli occupation of the Gaza Strip and the West Bank of the Jordan, which was especially intense from 1987 to 1990.

52.   Pike, "Societal Framework."

53.   Ibid.

54.   Ibid.

55.   Center for Army Lessons Learned (CALL), "Chapter 2: Civil Military Operations—Civil Affairs, Topic C: Cultural Issues in Iraq," in *Operation Iraqi Freedom (OIF)*, CAAT II Initial Impressions Report (IIR) No. 04–13 (Fort Leavenworth, KS: Center for Army Lessons Learned, May 2004). Online at <http://www.globalsecurity.org/military/library/report/call/call_04-13_chap01-c.htm> (as of 28 February 2006).

56.   Ibid.

57.   Ibid.

58.   Pike, "Societal Framework."

59.   Glen Fisher, *Mindsets: The Role of Culture and Perception in International Relations*, 2d edition (Yarmouth, ME: Intercultural Press, Inc., 1997), 72.

Chapter 4

Incorporating Cultural Awareness into US Military Training and Doctrine

Culture might be the best guide to understanding the intentions of both adversaries and allies on the battlefield. The cultural awareness model discussed here provides a means of acquiring knowledge of foreign cultures on the battlefield. However, to incorporate such understanding on the battlefield, training and doctrine must first include it. This chapter explains how to expand the cultural awareness model through a process of building cultural understanding and cultural competence. As explained in chapter 2 (see figure 1), cultural understanding is a higher level of cultural awareness that includes insights into the thought processes, motivating factors, and other issues that directly support the military decision-making process. Cultural competence is the highest level of cultural awareness, representing the fusion of cultural understanding with cultural intelligence to allow for focused insight into planning and decision-making for current and future military operations.[1] Cultural competence can be achieved only with adequate cultural intelligence—intelligence gathering that actively seeks information on the adversary's culture and the influences of this culture on decision-making. An intelligence-gathering process that considers cultural factors in a way that provides an effective basis for military planning is needed to support military operations. The chapter begins by defining the need for greater cultural awareness in training and doctrine. It then discusses some recommendations, as well as ongoing initiatives currently underway, designed to incorporate cultural awareness into US military doctrine and training.

The Need for Cultural Awareness in Training and Doctrine

The goal of providing soldiers and leaders with adequate preparation and an appropriate level of expectations before they enter the battlespace drives the need to incorporate cultural awareness into military training and doctrine. Such preparation will help personnel avoid the kinds of confusion and disappointment that can occur. Incorporating cultural awareness into training and doctrine will not eliminate the need to adjust and learn in the field, but it can help soldiers and leaders manage their expectations as they enter into an operation and allow for a more gradual "cultural learning curve."

A notional illustration of how cultural awareness training can help manage expectations is shown in figure 9.[2] In the figure, the level of soldiers' expectations is shown on the y-axis, while the level of cultural awareness and understanding is depicted on the x-axis.

The U-shaped line depicts the slope of expectations experienced by many soldiers in Iraq who did not receive much if any prior training relevant to

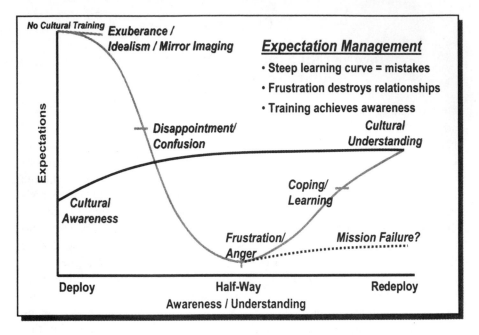

Figure 9. Cultural awareness and expectation management.

cultural awareness. Soldiers' initial exuberance and idealism, coupled with little to no cultural awareness, left many feeling disappointed and confused. Without prior understanding of key cultural factors, many soldiers initially drew conclusions about Iraqi culture based on their own cultural frame of reference, that is, assuming that Iraqis had attitudes, expectations, needs, and behavioral patterns similar to those of Americans. This process is called "mirror imaging" and is a common syndrome among people working outside their own familiar environment.[3] As soldiers became aware of the significant differences between American and Iraqi culture, the result for many was frustration, anger, and "culture shock." Culture shock is a term used to describe the anxiety and physical and emotional discomfort that can occur when a person moves to an unfamiliar environment.

Over time, the vast majority of soldiers have learned to moderate their expectations, managing to cope, and, eventually for some, gaining cultural understanding. However, in the meantime, many have lost productivity.[4] Moreover, the frustration and anger that result from false expectations and culture shock can contribute to mission failure. False expectations, such as those depicted in the figure, are a symptom of poor training, and only a dedicated training program in cultural awareness can overcome them.

The potential impact of cultural awareness training is indicated by the gently sloping upward curve, which shows the process through which soldiers deploy with a certain level of cultural awareness, thus lowering their expectations to a more realistic level. Gradually, these expectations might rise slightly as the soldiers gain true cultural understanding. This curve is gradual, however, producing no jolting disappointments or reversals of expectations. By adapting to a different sense of cultural logic before deployment, soldiers are less likely to perceive foreign behaviors as capricious and unpredictable. As a result, soldiers can experience less anxiety and can better cope with the unfamiliar.[5] Training that incorporates the cultural awareness model can facilitate this adaptation.

Cultural awareness gained in peacetime supports not only decisive combat operations, but stability and reconstruction operations as well. Cultural awareness is particularly important when US soldiers are involved in a "three-block war" in which troops are engaged in a spectrum of operations from humanitarian missions, to peacekeeping and peace enforcement operations, to full-blown combat—possibly within the space of three city blocks.[6] Entering a foreign culture with proper training and preparation will help soldiers navigate through these complexities.

To successfully wage a "three-block war," soldiers must be able to transition between its three elements as smoothly and seamlessly as possible—through the lens of cultural awareness. To do this, military leaders need an understanding of situational awareness as it relates to culture on the battlefield. Mission success depends on the ability to bridge the cultural gaps both in warfighting and in intelligence gathering.

From a military perspective, cultural intelligence provides a means to capture the nonmilitary elements of information that are especially relevant in stability and support operations. Cultural intelligence is the process of incorporating cultural factors in the intelligence cycle and the estimate analysis to support the commander's decision-making process. Cultural intelligence is not a separate intelligence discipline, but a fused product of all-source analysis. Cultural intelligence data is collected primarily through human intelligence (HUMINT) and signals intelligence (SIGINT), but can come from any source regarding the social, political, and economic aspects of governments and civil populations, their demographics, structures, capabilities, organizations, people, and events.[7] While some aspects of cultural intelligence fall specifically within the realm of intelligence collection and production, commanders, by using a baseline of cultural awareness, can direct the collection of appropriate raw cultural data that is then processed with other data (geographic, military, technical, and so forth). The focus of cultural intelligence must be at the tactical level to provide the greatest direct benefit to the soldier in combat.

Below is a discussion of some strategies for integrating cultural awareness into military training and operations.[8] First it looks at the training of soldiers and leaders through professional military education (PME) and AOR-specific predeployment training at the unit level. Then it considers how cultural awareness can be integrated into Army doctrine to facilitate planning and decision-making processes, specifically with regard to the intelligence preparation of the battlefield (IPB), the commander's estimate and the deliberate planning process (at the operational level), and the military decision-making process (at the tactical level).

Figure 10 provides an overview of the changes required. The model shows pathways to integrate systematically cultural considerations—horizontally and vertically—into US military training and operations.

The incorporation of cultural factors into military training and doctrine can support effects-based operations (EBO), which can be described as offensive, defensive, stability, and support operations planned and executed to achieve the commander's desired effect on a threat element, civil leader (tribal, ethnic, or governmental), or population group. "EBO achieves the commander's desired effect through the synchronized, sequential, or simultaneous application of leadership, maneuver, firepower, and information."[9]

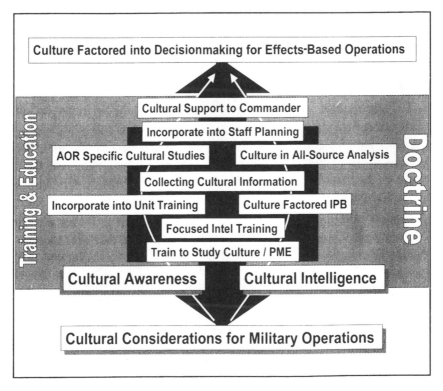

Figure 10. Changes in training and doctrine required to achieve cultural competence.

Integrating Cultural Awareness into Military Training

In today's operational environment, especially that of stability and reconstruction operations, military leaders must understand the actors who can affect their operations. These actors include enemy forces, insurgent forces, noncompliant forces, the civil population, local leaders, and others.[10] Commanders can no longer plan military operations against a military force and not consider the second- and third-order effects that such military actions will have on the civil population and the local leaders with whom they seek favorable relations. Soldiers require cultural knowledge to assist with on-the-ground decision-making. Such awareness will further enable the United States not only to win the tactical fight, but the overall campaign as well.

Soldiers and leaders can acquire the necessary cultural understanding through training that incorporates the kinds of cultural awareness lessons described in chapters 2 and 3. As described in the cultural awareness model in chapter 2, the US military needs to know what influences a given culture, what the cultural variations are in terms of behaviors and values, and how these influences and variations manifest themselves in outward behaviors. Chapter 3 illustrated how these elements come into play in Middle Eastern culture, particularly in Iraq.

Figure 11 represents a modification of the cultural awareness pyramid (introduced in chapter 2) to illustrate how different kinds of training are needed to provide different levels of cultural awareness, and to support soldiers during various stages of the training-deployment-operations cycle.

As indicated by the figure, soldiers require cultural competence to support operations. Cultural competence results from the intimate knowledge of an adversary's (or ally's) motivation, intent, will, and tactical methods. The US military needs soldiers (and Marines) who can deal with a diversity of peoples and cultures, tolerate ambiguity, take initiative, and ask questions.[11] US soldiers "must notice small differences and pick up nuances, developing the sensitivity to see key indicators."[12] Only by understanding an enemy's thought process can better-educated analyses be conducted of potential actions and reactions. The process of acquiring cultural competence must begin long before deployment. This preparation will allow leaders to think and adapt faster than the enemy, and allow soldiers to thrive in an environment of uncertainty, ambiguity, and unfamiliar cultural circumstances.[13]

Training Initiatives Currently Underway

Changes to incorporate cultural awareness into military training are already underway at the installation level, at training centers, and in select PME courses. Many military leaders are taking the initiative and using the limited resources available to teach and integrate cultural awareness in their predeployment training.

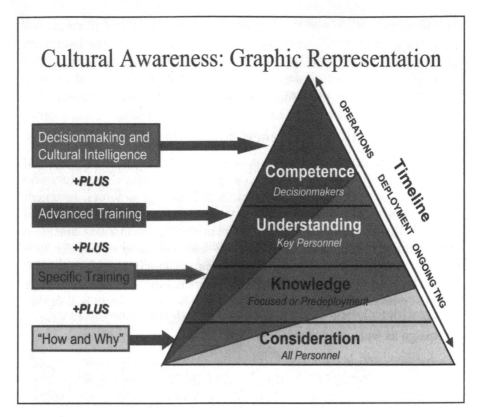

Figure 11. Training considerations and the pyramid of cultural awareness.

Since mid-2003, JRTCs and NTCs have offered an Iraq- or Afghanistan-focused block of instruction that includes "engagement" or negotiation training, media training, and cultural awareness training to the key leadership of its rotating units. Many Active and Reserve Component leaders have modified their predeployment training, and enlisted the help of local colleges and universities to provide native Arabic speakers and subject matter experts to provide cultural training to their soldiers. The Command and General Staff College teaches courses specifically designed for field grade officers deploying to Afghanistan or Iraq. Additionally, a number of Active Component divisions (especially those scheduled to return to Iraq or Afghanistan) have invited subject matter experts and Foreign Area Officers from JRTC, Defense Language Institute (DLI), and the institutional Army to visit their installations to teach cultural awareness to soldiers.

Additional Changes Needed to Standardize Cultural Awareness Training Across the Army

Beyond the initiatives already underway, the Army needs additional changes above the local level to formalize and standardize cultural awareness training. Cultural awareness must be formally integrated into PME courses and the Non-commissioned Officer Education System (NCOES). Recognizing the inherent shortfalls of cultural competence within the force, the Army has recently begun to study ways to formalize the integration of Arabic and Islamic cultural awareness into its PME system. In April 2005, the Commanding General (CG), Training and Doctrine Command (TRADOC), outlined the requirement for "leaders who can understand and apply knowledge of cultures" to facilitate the creation of agile and joint expeditionary capable forces. He established broad, overarching guidance that recognizes "cultural training as a Common Core for all levels of PME and directed an emphasis on the instruction in all NCOES and company-grade officer PME courses." This directive describes learning objectives for Arab and Islamic cultural training at every level of PME for officers, warrant officers, and noncommissioned officers (NCOs), and further directs the Commander, Combined Arms Center (CAC) and Fort Leavenworth to publish implementation guidance to "establish broad, overarching guidance on culture training to all TRADOC schools." This guidance lists the "key tenets of the Arab World" that must be addressed through cultural training for leaders, respective of their specific roles and responsibilities.[14] These include:

- Geography.
- History.
- Religious composition.
- Political structures.
- Islam (history, tenets, major branches, and the role of Islam in Arab politics).
- Arab/Islamic customs and social norms (verbal/nonverbal communications, etiquette, and roles of gender in society).
- Governance and laws (secular, religious, and tribal).[15]

By incorporating cultural awareness training into the institutional Army through changes to PME, NCOES, combat training centers, and doctrine, the Army is on its way to developing leaders with the ability to provide Joint Task Force (JTF) and Combined Force Land Component Command (CFLCC) commanders and staffs with accurate assessments of the local military, political, religious, and commercial situation.[16]

The Foreign Area Officer (FAO) program should be expanded to ensure a sufficient number of military officers are trained in this area. In addition, the

US military must ensure an adequate number of military officers are trained as Foreign Area Officers (FAOs). FAOs are commissioned officers from all services who have regional expertise, language competency, and political-military awareness. FAOs serve as attachés or security assistance officers at US embassies, to implement US national security strategy, often as the sole DOD representative in country. FAOs may also serve on joint staffs to provide a regional and cultural perspective for planning and execution of military operations and to advise senior leaders.[17]

In a September 2004 *Proceedings* article, retired General Robert Scales discusses building military capacity for what he describes as "Culture-Centric Warfare" through "a cadre of global scouts, well educated, with a penchant for languages and a comfort with strange and distant places."[18] As warriors who provide focused regional expertise to the joint warfighter, Army FAOs are today's "global scouts" and are at the heart of this culture-centric issue. Through their training and in-country experience, Army FAOs "have knowledge of political-military affairs; have familiarity with the political, cultural, sociological, economic, and geographic factors of the countries and regions in which they are stationed; and have professional proficiency in one or more of the dominant languages in their regions of expertise."[19] Today, Army FAOs operate decisively in uncertain environments, often independently, and serve as valuable force multipliers to commanders and senior leaders from the tactical to the strategic level.

In the past, FAOs were not deemed as essential as they are today. Field grade officers who performed nonoperational missions with the State Department as attachés and political-military officers or served in security cooperation roles were not held in the same esteem as those who served in multiple battalion- and brigade-level assignments. As a result, FAO promotion rates were consistently below the averages; therefore, the Army has continued to face shortages of qualified FAOs.

To rectify this situation and meet the evolving need for more FAOs in the Army and throughout the military, in April 2005 Deputy Secretary of Defense Paul Wolfowitz reissued DOD Directive 1315.17, Military Department Foreign Area Officer (FAO) Programs. In doing so, he states:

> To achieve national security objectives and success in current and future operations, including the war on Terrorism, the US Armed Forces shall be prepared to conduct military operations in a variety of conditions around the world. The Combatant Commands shall have the requisite warfighting capabilities to achieve success on the nonlinear battlefields of the future. These critical warfighting capabilities include foreign language proficiency and detailed knowledge of the regions of the world gained through in-depth study and personal experience. Additionally, these capabilities facilitate close and continuous military-diplomatic interaction with foreign governments and, in particular, with their defense and military establishments, which is

essential to developing and maintaining constructive mutually supportive, bilateral and multilateral military activities and relationships across the range of operations.[20]

To maintain a sufficient number of FAOs in both the Active and Reserve Components, Wolfowitz asked the secretaries of the military departments to develop a detailed action plan that includes training the number of military officers required to meet their FAO needs and provides both a viable career path and the opportunity for FAO promotion into the general officer ranks.[21] The Army FAO program will continue to evolve along with the rest of the Army and the world in which the US military operates. An improved FAO program can significantly contribute to the planning and execution of transitions to and from hostilities, as well as support DOD plans to improve HUMINT capabilities and strategic communications.

Integrating Cultural Awareness into Military Doctrine

Army doctrine describes how the Army intends to fight. It reflects the "fundamental principles by which the military forces or elements thereof guide their actions in support of national objectives. It is authoritative, but requires judgment in application."[22] As described earlier, US joint doctrine acknowledges that cultural differences among coalition partners may impact the mission. However, current Army doctrine does not consider the impact of culture on internal mission planning, nor does it provide its commanders with a comprehensive and structured approach to cultural considerations in the operational planning process.

The development of Army doctrine is determined by the operational concept formed by historical experience; military theory; and political, economic, and other factors that influence National Security and Military Strategies. Lessons learned from Operation Enduring Freedom (OEF) and Operation Iraqi Freedom (OIF) indicate that improvements are required in "institutional preparation in language, as well as political, ideological, and cultural training"; culture has begun to receive some attention in military doctrine. In these documents, culture often includes common elements such as beliefs, values, and religion, but also physical elements such as buildings and infrastructure.[23] An example of this is evident in the June 2005 edition of FM 1, *The Army*, which states:

> In the new security environment, cultural awareness has become one of the most important knowledge areas for Army leaders. Army leaders develop their knowledge of major world cultures and learn how those cultures affect military operations. The Army's rich mix of soldiers' backgrounds and cultures is a natural enabler of cultural awareness. . . . This knowledge helps them become more self-aware and adaptive.[24]

Additionally, future revisions of FM 3-0, *Operations*; FM 5-0, *Army Planning and Orders Production*; and FM 3-07.22, *Counterinsurgency*, will provide an increased emphasis on cultural awareness.[25] This emphasis must go beyond cultural awareness as it refers to political and ideological beliefs, values, religion, language preparation, and whether cultural differences among coalition partners may impact the mission, and must incorporate cultural awareness into the intelligence preparation of the battlefield process, the commander's estimate, and the military decision-making process.

The Need for Cultural Awareness in Intelligence-Gathering

One needs to understand the role of information operations (IO) during OIF to understand how to incorporate cultural awareness into the intelligence gathering process. This analysis will help identify gaps in the intelligence-gathering process that could be bridged by improved cultural awareness. We draw on an assessment conducted by LTC John Strycula, who served in Iraq for twelve months with the 4th Infantry Division as the deputy G2.[26] The analysis used Army-defined criteria to assess the effectiveness of key intelligence tasks during OIF. Relevant tasks were identified using FM 7-15, *Army Universal Task List (AUTL)*, which provides a standard doctrinal foundation and catalogue of the Army's tactical collective tasks, including intelligence.[27] Criteria for assessing these activities were derived from FM 2-0, *Intelligence*, which states that "intelligence products must be timely, relevant, accurate, and predictive."[28] The criteria for evaluating intelligence support are defined as follows:

- Timeliness: Was the reporting and dissemination of the intelligence timely enough to support proactive information operations and allow quicker decisions than the adversary?
- Relevance: Was the intelligence collected and disseminated to support IO pertinent and applicable to the commander's critical information requirements (CCIR) and IO mission planning?
- Accuracy/Sufficient Detail: Was the intelligence output accurate and of a sufficient level of fidelity to support IO planning at multiple levels of command?
- Predictiveness: Did the intelligence support to IO enable the commander and his staff to anticipate key enemy events or reactions and develop corresponding counteractions?

These criteria were used to provide a qualitative assessment of whether intelligence support during OIF was timely enough to support proactive IO, pertinent to the commander's intelligence requirements, accurate with sufficient detail, and capable of helping the commander and staff anticipate key events. The evaluation focused on the intelligence support provided to the Combined Force Land Component Command (CFLCC) and the Combined

Joint Task Force-7 (CJTF-7), but personal experiences at the division and brigade level also influenced the evaluations.[29]

The results of the analysis are shown in figure 12.[30] The left-hand column of the figure details the primary intelligence support to IO tasks that are defined in the AUTL. The next two columns represent the evaluations of those tasks conducted during the major combat operations (MCO) and stability and support operations (SASO) phases, respectively. The final column provides the criteria or rationale that caused that specific task to be evaluated as either green (G), yellow (Y), or red (R). To further delineate the results of the analysis, the appraisal has been separated into MCO and SASO phases of the conflict. All ratings in the figure represent Strycula's subjective assessment of the intelligence support to IO during OIF.

If a task was judged to satisfy all four of these criteria, then it was assessed to be successful and labeled green (G). However, if a task only accomplished three of the four criteria, it was evaluated as marginally or partially successful and coded yellow (Y). If the intelligence accomplished only two of the four criteria, then it was evaluated to be unsatisfactory and coded red (R). In addition, because accuracy is arguably the most important

UNIVERSAL TASK LIST OF INTEL SUPPORT TO IO	MCO	SASO	WHY
IDENTIFY ENEMY C2 NODES	G	G	EFFECTIVE
IDENTIFY ENEMY COMMUNICATION SYSTEMS	G	Y	PREDICTIVE
IDENTIFY ENEMY COMPUTER SYSTEMS	G	Y	PREDICTIVE
IDENTIFY TARGETS FOR ELECTRONIC ATTACK	G	G	EFFECTIVE
PROVIDE INTELLIGENCE SUPPORT TO PSYOPS	G	Y	PREDICTIVE
IDENTIFY PROFILES OF KEY ADVERSARY LEADERS	G	●	ACCURACY
DESCRIBE ADVERSARY DECISIONMAKING PROCESSES AND BIASES	Y	●	ACCURACY
IDENTIFY THE ADVERSARY PERCEPTION OF THE MILITARY SITUATION	Y	●	ACCURACY
IDENTIFY POPULATION DEMOGRAPHICS, ATTITUDES, AND BEHAVIORS	●	●	ACCURACY
IDENTIFY LOCATION AND BIASES OF NATIONAL AND INTERNATIONAL MEDIA	G	Y	EFFECTIVE

Figure 12. Evaluating intelligence support to IO during OIF.

criteria of the four, this was set as the critical evaluation criteria. Therefore, if the intelligence was judged to be inaccurate, then regardless of the ratings on the other criteria, that category of intelligence support would be rated unsuccessful or red (R).

The first five intelligence tasks listed in figure 12 are the primary tasks associated with intelligence support to offensive IO. The evaluation seems to indicate that intelligence provided overall effective support to offensive IO. Knowledge of the specific e-mail addresses of Iraqi army commanding generals used to transmit capitulation messages is an example of the exceptional intelligence support to this offensive IO task.[31] Also, the years of collection in support of both Operation Northern and Southern Watch provided vast and detailed information that enabled electronic attacks at both the operational and tactical levels to be extremely successful.[32] Additionally, the 1st Information Operations Command (IOC) leveraged the intelligence collected during twelve years to create thorough and informative products that detailed the communication networks, nodes, and methods.

The next three intelligence AUTL tasks define the intelligence that describes the identities, propensities, and decision-making styles of the adversarial leaders. The assessment indicates that the Intelligence Battlefield Operating System (IBOS) struggled to satisfy these intelligence requirements, especially during the SASO phases of the conflict.[33] The IPB produced by the 1st IOC in support of the MCO on Saddam's decision-making system was very comprehensive, detailing all of Saddam's closest advisers and their relationships and responsibilities within his decision-making and command and control system. It further described the key personnel and the methods of communications and command and control of both the Republican Guard and Regular Army forces. However, the level of detail and accuracy greatly decreased following the transition to phase IV (stability and support) operations. For example, CJTF-7 continued to target exclusively the original Top 55 Most Wanted Iraqis nearly six months after the end of combat operations, despite the fact that few of the original Most Wanted had any intelligence reporting indicating involvement in the insurgency. This unmodified list is a very telling example of the struggles the IBOS had in grasping and identifying the insurgency leadership during the SASO phase. The 1st IOC IPB products produced after the beginning of the SASO phase also demonstrated the difficulty the IBOS had in identifying the adversarial leaders. Furthermore, the intelligence provided on their decision-making system was limited; however, their products did include neutral and friendly leaders and a partial analysis of their command and control system.

The IBOS had difficulty providing information regarding the population demographics, attitudes, and behaviors. The intelligence required to support this category implies more information than the raw numbers found in the *CIA World Fact Book*; still, an understanding is needed of the effects these demographics and details will have on operations. This information falls into the category of cultural intelligence as previously defined.

In terms of the successes, it appears that the IBOS satisfied those ten intelligence requirements that have been historically levied on the intelligence collection system or those that were satisfied by conventional intelligence requirements. Specifically, the IBOS succeeded and even excelled in providing the technical intelligence support requirements to IO, such as identifying communications methods and nodes.[34] These successes can also be attributed to the technical leaning of the intelligence collection system.

On the other hand, the IBOS struggled with the human or cognitive intelligence tasks, such as providing cultural intelligence and information on the adversary's decision-making system.[35] A review of the tasks that the IBOS failed to satisfy suggests problems especially with the SASO phase of operations, when the human, cultural, and intelligence requirements come to the fore. The IBOS did not emphasize the collection and identification of many of the secondary political figures and tribal leaders during the years before OIF. The Land Information Warfare Activity, the predecessor to 1st IOC, states that the IBOS must shift its focus from the technical requirements to the human dimension prior to the operational transition to SASO to facilitate the phase IV (SASO) pre-execution planning.[36]

Research further indicates there were two primary causes for the IBOS breakdowns.[37] First was the poor integration of IO analysis within the battlestaff's IPB process. Many of the key IO intelligence requirements were not identified anywhere outside of IO doctrine. This isolation of IO analysis and the failure to highlight its information needs during the battlestaff's IPB process caused the IBOS to be oblivious to these requirements. Another cause for the IBOS failures was the lack of detailed and complete cultural intelligence during the IPB process and IO planning. The lack of cultural intelligence within the IPB process to support effective psychological and civil-military operations was identified as a deficiency in both the 3d Infantry and 82d Airborne Divisions' After Actions Reports.[38] Both stated that they needed a better understanding of the cultural, religious, and ethnic compositions to plan IO and predict the reactions of the population.[39] This information gap and an understanding of its effects on both friendly and enemy operations became a problem not only for IO, but for the larger IPB process as well. The bottom line is that the Coalition did not take into consideration the possible culture reactions of the enemy, adversary, and neutral population. The battlestaffs focused on the tactical reactions of the enemy and did not consider the Iraqi reactions to US operations based on their culture.[40]

Probably the most notable trend illustrated by figure 12 is the overall decrease in the effectiveness and accuracy of intelligence support to IO during the SASO phase compared to the MCO phase, including poorer support for many of the tasks the IBOS effectively supported during the MCO phase, like

Table 5. Shift in Operations That Must Take Place During SASO.

Shortfalls Particularly Pronounced in Phase IV

Warfighting Operations	Stability Operations
Conventional military operations	Administration, information operations, and conventional military operations
Attrition of fighting power of Military Units– Decisive Action	Management of Perception of Civil Government, Population–Stability
Targets: Humans and Machines	Targets: Hearts and Minds of Government, Tribal and Religious Leaders
Locating, tracking, identifying, targeting, and killing physical objects (C4ISR)	Locating, tracking, identifying, and influencing minds (reason) and hearts (emotions)
Physical Sciences	Social and Cognitive Sciences
Physical Sensing	Civil Collection, Sensing
Target ID, Tracking	Perception ID, Tracking
Physical Situational Awareness	Cognitive Situational Awareness

electronic warfare, suffered in the transition between MCO and SASO. The technical focus of the IBOS had difficulty shifting to understand the asymmetric and adaptive enemy in Iraq during SASO. Table 5 articulates the cognitive changes that must take place in the transition from major combat operations to stability operations.[41]

Ultimately, the military must shift from the physical science aspects of war to those of social and cognitive sciences. The latter type of war is won through the management of perceptions, building trust, and reading intentions.[42] This is a thinking person's game—it is the cultural phase of war. The United States cannot win in this environment unless it understands the culture.

Changes Needed to Integrate Cultural Awareness into IPB Doctrine

The kinds of issues identified in the previous section can be addressed through changes to doctrine. This section will discuss ways to expand IPB doctrine to include cultural factors. Table 6 shows the steps in the current IPB doctrine[43] along with recommended additions designed to address cultural factors (indicated by a "YES" in the right-hand column).

The steps in the current doctrinal IPB process focus on a technical understanding of the adversary. Highlighted are the additional intelligence factors

Table 6. Recommended Additions to Doctrine to Achieve Cultural Intelligence.

Step or Substep	Need to Add to Current Process?
Step 1: Define the Battlefield Environment	
Effective in describing the characteristics of the battlefield	
Step 2: Describe the Battlefield Effects	
Terrain analysis	
Weather analysis	
Infrastructure analysis	YES
Cultural intelligence analysis	YES
Other characteristics of the battlefield	
Step 3: Evaluate the Threat	
Update or create threat models	
Identify threat capabilities	
Identify threat decisionmaking system	
Step 4: Determine Enemy Courses of Action	
Identify enemy's likely objectives and endstates	
Identify enemy's decision points and triggers for those decisions	YES
Identify the full set of COAs available to the threat	
Evaluate and prioritize each course of action	

that need to be added to make the intelligence analysis more complete. The addition of these factors would improve intelligence support to IO and would enhance the overall IPB process by making it more comprehensive.

The first recommendation is to add a subparagraph specifically dedicated to the cultural intelligence factors and a discussion of their effects on both friendly and enemy operations. Such a paragraph was not required in the past because the US understanding of an adversary's culture was based on a view of the enemy through the former Soviet Union doctrine. Now, as the United States continues to operate in the contemporary operating environment (COE), the adversaries are much more varied and adaptive in terms of motivation and doctrine.[44]

By incorporating cultural awareness into intelligence-gathering, the result would be "cultural intelligence," i.e., intelligence derived from all sources regarding the social, political, and economic aspects of governments and civil populations, their demographics, structures, capabilities, organizations, people, and events. Table 7 shows the key components of cultural awareness.[45]

Table 7. Cultural Intelligence Categories.

Intelligence derived from all sources regarding the social, political, and economic aspects of governments and civil populations, their demographics, structures, capabilities, organizations, people, and events.					
1. Physical Setting	2. Political	3. *Socio-Cultural*	4. Economic	5. Media	6. External
• Topography and Underlying Terrain	• State Institutions and Structures	• *Population Demographics*	• Resources and production	• Media Sources and Channels	• International Actors, Organizations
• Boundaries	• Government Administration (Actors)	• *Population Culture*	• Commerce and Trade • Finance and Transportation	• Media Controllers (Actors)	Nongovernmental Organizations (NGOs)
• Physical Compositions and Neighborhoods	• Political Organizations (Actors)		• State Roles • Foreign Roles • Power Structure		
• Civil Infrastructure • Buildings	• Criminal Organizations				

Each of the areas in table 7 can be further developed and refined based on the requirements needed to inform the decision-making process. Table 8 expands on the sociocultural category to define further intelligence needs in this area. The areas listed draw on the cultural awareness model presented in chapter 2. FM 2-01.3, *Intelligence Preparation of the Battlefield*, does not currently specify many of these important factors. These factors are also relevant for training as well.

Table 8 illustrates recommended cultural intelligence factors that should be added to the second step of the IPB process, helping planners and intelligence personnel to identify mission essential facts. A generic guideline like the one shown in the table can be created to identify those factors normally important to military operations. All of these factors affect the thinking and motivation of individuals or groups, and make up the cultural terrain of the battlespace.

Doctrine might distinguish between those aspects of culture that are not subject to frequent change, such as a culture's language, history, or major social groups, and those that change more often, such as local power structures or the current issues dividing the society. Home station training might effectively focus on those types of information that are not likely to change prior to deployment. The focus in theater could be on those issues and aspects of culture that are subject to change over the course of a rotation.

Table 8. Cultural Intelligence Factors That Should Be Better Addressed in Doctrine.

• LANGUAGES	• LITERACY RATES/EDUCATION LEVELS
• HISTORY, REGION, AND NATION STATE	• DIASPORAS
• RELIGIONS (BELIEFS AND INSTITUTIONS)	• SOCIAL ROLES OF POPULATION SEG-MENTS (WOMEN, ELDERS)
• SOCIAL GROUPS	
–ETHNIC, RACE, TRIBAL/CLAN	• CULTURAL VARIATIONS AND MANIFESTATIONS
–RELIGIOUS AFFILIATIONS	
–ECONOMIC PARTNERSHIPS	
–LEADERS, ELITES, FOLLOWERS	• COGNITIVE DOMAIN
(RELIGIOUS, TRIBAL, CIVIL, BUSINESS)	–NEGOTIATING
–ARMED GROUPS	–PERSISTENT, HISTORICALLY BASED
(PRO, NEUTRAL, INSURGENT)	–PERCEPTIONS, OUTLOOKS, TEMPERAMENTS
–CUSTOMS, ATTITUDES, SOCIAL TABOOS	–ORGANIZATIONAL BEHAVIOR (POLITICAL, ECONOMIC, SOCIAL)
–COHESIVE AND DIVISIVE ISSUES IN THE COMMUNITY	• CULTURALLY SIGNIFICANT LOCATIONS
	• DATES, HOLIDAYS, AND EVENTS

> *MANY IMPORTANT FACTORS NOT SPECIFIED IN FM 2–01.3*
> *DESCRIBE THEIR EFFECTS ON THE BATTLEFIELD*

Additionally, the effects and impacts that an adversary's culture will have on their decisions and tactics must be incorporated into the analysis of the enemy. The "Other Characteristics" paragraph in the IPB manual shows that the analyst should consider other factors that may influence an operation. Unfortunately, this "Other Characteristics" paragraph does not currently contain any specific cultural intelligence factors or examples to help guide analysis and drive intelligence collection. To fully develop cultural intelligence and integrate it into the larger IPB process, a specific listing of relevant factors need to be defined to help determine what factors are significant. More importantly, a discussion of how these factors will influence friendly and adversary operations should also be included. Most intelligence analysts working on division and brigade combat team battlestaffs do not have a sufficient cultural or sociology background to determine the relevant factors and their effects independently. Once the list of the militarily relevant cultural intelligence factors has been determined, their effects on operations must be defined. The discussion and definitions must attempt to explain the effects of cultural factors on both friendly and adversary operations.

The final area that needs expanded within the IPB process is a framework for analyzing the adversary's leaders and their decision-making system. Step 3 of the current IPB process focuses on evaluating the threat by creating threat models or templates to determine the adversary's capabilities; however, there is no mention of an analysis of the adversary's leaders and their decision-making system. An analytical framework must be developed not only to analyze the enemy's military leaders, but also to analyze adversarial, neutral, and friendly government, civilian, and military leaders. This information is essential "to get inside the target's head and understanding their leadership style."[46] This is critically important as the United States continues to face an increasingly asymmetric and adaptive enemy. Moreover, an analysis of the decision-making system will further the development of estimated enemy decision points and indicators associated with those decisions, and help identify vulnerabilities for IO to exploit.

One possible construct for conducting an analysis of the adversary leaders and their decision-making system is to use this simple four-step process during step 3 of the IPB process, "Evaluate the Threat." Table 9 shows such a framework. This framework will identify who the decisionmakers are, define their decision-making style, describe their command and control system, and most importantly, identify the vulnerabilities in the system that the United States

Table 9. Steps in Analyzing the Adversary's Decision-making System.

- Step 1–Identify and Describe the Decision-makers
  - Who are the decision-makers (threat, adversary, neutral)?
  - What is their basis of power/leadership?
  - What are their sources of information?
  - What are their goals or endstates?
- Step 2–Describe the Decision-making Style
  - What is the leaders decision-making style?
  - Who are the subordinates of the decision-maker?
  - What is the decision-maker's authority?
- Step 3–Identify and Describe the Command and Control System
  - Where are the command and control nodes?
  - What is the method for receiving information and transmitting decisions?
  - In what form does the information travel?
- Step 4–Where Are the Vulnerabilities That We Can Exploit?
  - What methods of IO can we use to influence?
  - Where can we get inside the adversary's decision cycle?
  - What can we effect?
    - The decision-maker, his decision-making style, or the information?

should exploit. This four-step analysis of the adversary's decision-making system will ensure that a comprehensive view of the enemy is undertaken.

This kind of framework can guide and focus the analyst to consider all three information age warfare domains of conflict as defined by Admiral Arthur Cebrowski[47] in *Understanding Information Age Warfare.*[48] These domains are the cognitive, informational, and physical. The intent is to develop a simple model that can be applied to a military or political leader during an MCO, but also be employed to analyze a tribal, religious, or insurgent leader in a SASO environment. It is important to develop a universal analysis model that can be equally applied across the full spectrum of combat so the US military does not perpetuate the decline in intelligence support to IO that was seen during OIF in the transition from MCO to SASO.

The first step in evaluating the adversary decision-making system is to identify the leaders and decision-makers. It is important to realize that the identified leaders are not necessarily or by default the decision-makers. This is especially true in a SASO environment where the tribal or religious leader may not have decision-making authority. A full perception of the leadership encompasses an understanding of the leader's basis of power, sources of information, and individual and group goals and objectives. This step of the model is designed to analyze the cognitive domain of the decision-making system. The cognitive domain is "where perceptions, awareness, understanding, beliefs and values . . . and where . . . decisions are made. . . . This is the domain of intangibles: leadership, morale, unit cohesion, . . . and . . . situational awareness. . . ."[49]

The second step is to describe the decision-making style that is being utilized. For example, are the leader's decisions final, as in a dictatorship or military organization, or are decisions made by consensus, as in a religious council of clerics or Ulema. This step represents an understanding and analysis of the informational domain of information age warfare. This knowledge is critical to identify vulnerabilities that can be exploited by IO. To understand further the decision-making style, the staff must identify the subordinates the leader controls and explain his authority over those subordinates. The informational domain is arguably the most important to understand to effectively plan, execute, and assess IO. In addition to being the most crucial, it is also probably the most difficult intelligence task to collect.

The third step focuses on the physical domain, particularly command and control issues. This domain of information age warfare focuses on where and how the entities transfer information. It includes defining the communications networks and the forms of the information.[50] This aspect of intelligence support to IO has traditionally been a strongpoint for the IBOS. This again is because both the intelligence collection and analysis systems have been optimized to provide the technical information required to conduct this type of analysis. To understand fully the physical domain of the decision-making system, the IBOS must not only identify the location of command and control nodes, but must also identify the media and the specific form the information takes. This analysis step is vaguely defined to make the model apply to the analysis of a military commander's command and control system or one of a tribal or clerical leader.

The final step involves determining where vulnerabilities exist that can be exploited. As the three domains of information age warfare are analyzed using this simple model, the vulnerabilities for exploitation are clearly exhibited, and the commander can then determine the best way to exploit these vulnerabilities. For example, he may decide to appeal to the tribal leader's economic objectives by providing some additional work projects directly to the Shiekh and his tribe. Alternatively, he might decide to approach secondary tribal leaders with a similar plan, so they can lobby and ultimately influence the senior tribal leader's decision. The intent of this simple model is to provide a clear-cut framework to analyze the enemy's decision-making system and to identify the vulnerabilities that IO can exploit.

Table 10 shows how cultural intelligence can be applied to the IPB process.[51] The table shows an IPB that has been supplemented to include socio-cultural factors in addition to the traditional areas of physical terrain, enemy force dispositions, and aspects of infrastructure that influence and constrain symmetric force-on-force combat operations.[52]

The addition of the factors of cultural intelligence to IPB doctrine would enable and facilitate a more complete analysis of the enemy, adversary, and neutral leaders in the contemporary operating environment.

Changes Needed in the Deliberative Planning Process and Execution Phase

The incorporation of cultural factors in military training and doctrine can support effects-based operations (EBO), which, as noted earlier, refer to offensive, defensive, stability, and support operations planned and executed to achieve the commander's desired effect on a threat element, civil leader (tribal, ethnic, or governmental), or population group. EBO provides both a way of thinking about operations and a set of processes and procedures designed to improve planning, execution, and assessment of military operations. They provide a means of bridging the cultural gap, and the US military must be effects-based in everything it does.[53] Effects-based planning (a component of EBO) is a rational decision-making model that analyzes an adversary by examining the relationships among an adversary's political, military, economic, social, infrastructure, and information systems.

Deliberative Planning Process. Once the IPB process has been modified to incorporate cultural awareness factors, the deliberative planning process can then be adapted to incorporate cultural intelligence. Figure 13 provides a graphical representation of the deliberate planning process modified to incorporate cultural intelligence factors.[54]

Table 10. Example of a Modified IPB.

	Intelligence				Operations			
	Intelligence Preparation of the Battlefield (IPB)				Effects-based Operations (EBO)			
Analytic Elements	Terrain Analysis	Enemy Force	Infrastructure Analysis	Population Analysis	Administrative Operations	Information Operations	Security Operations	**Operation Elements**
Objects of Analysis	Natural Terrain	Enemy Force	Structures (physical and informational)	Civil Populations, Institutions	Civil Populations, Institutions	Information Flows and Content	Civil Populations, Opposition	**Object of Operations**
Example Components	Topography Hydrography Vegetation Barriers	Equipment Force Structure Order of Battle Intent Capabilities Timing	Buildings LOCs Information channels, nodes-telecom, media	Demography Populations Perceptions Norms Decision-making Style	Policy, laws, regs News Security PA CA	PSYOP CNO EW Physical	Patrols Searches Raids Direct Action	**Example Components**

Traditional IPB | Modified IPB

Cultural Intelligence

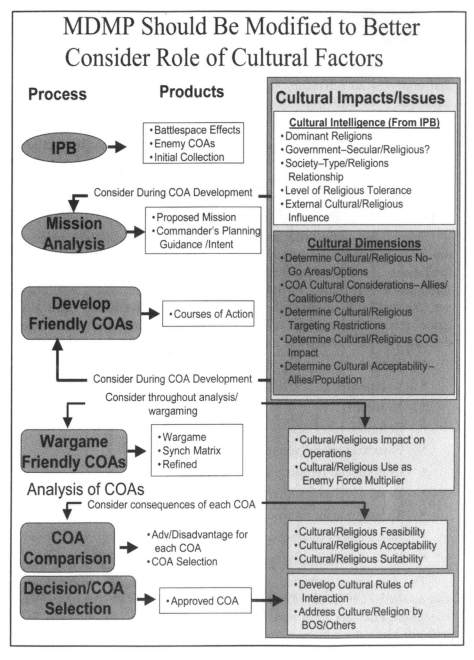

Figure 13. Deliberate planning process modified to incorporate cultural intelligence factors.

During the commander's estimate of the situation (CES) process, the intelligence planner determines enemy (or adversary) capabilities, limitations, intentions, and potential courses of action. During the Joint Intelligence Preparation of the Battlefield (JIPB), the intelligence planner, assisted by a cultural adviser or specialist (if available), must also gather relevant cultural and religious information. Based on the concepts discussed in this study, these cultural and religious factors must describe:

- The society.
- Its customs.
- Its values.
- Religious practices.
- External cultural and religious influences.
- Cultural and religious attitudes toward warfare.
- Level of religious tolerance.
- The significant historical cultural and religious tensions.
- International interactions.
- Decision-making styles.

The data, once collected, must be available during mission analysis and course of action development for consideration of its impact on plan execution. Planners must remember that these cultural and religious factors are likely to influence assumptions, constraints, restraints, implied tasks, and initial risk assessment. Cultural and religious factors contemplated during course of action development will influence actions considered to achieve mission success. Furthermore, identified negative impacts on feasibility, suitability, or acceptability should lead to course of action rejection or modification to mitigate the potential damaging effects.

The framework above is designed to ensure that military planners are aware of and consider culture and religion throughout the CES process. This model provides a comprehensive single-source compilation of the factors of cultural competence developed during the course of this study. The potential negative effects of culture and religion on mission planning and execution can be mitigated through additional staff support for the combatant commander, more detailed cultural rules of engagement for mission participants, and modification of joint doctrine to include a framework for considering culture and religion during the CES.[55]

Execution phase. With regard to strategic communications during the execution phases of military operations, the US military must understand the issues in friendly, failing, and failed states. The military needs to know who these states are and what their leaders and citizens believe. Only then can the military decide whom to address, what messages to communicate, and what media to employ (i.e., themes and messages, products, programs) to design

Cultural Competence Is Needed Across All Levels of War			
	Implications/How is Feature Manifested		
Dimensions of Cultural Variance	**Strategic** *National/Theater mission objectives, using diplomatic, economic, and military means to accomplish goals (policy)*	**Operational** *The organization of mid-level objectives into plans to accomplish strategic goals*	**Tactical** *The implementation of plans in terms of observable activity "on the ground"*
Behaviors The outward, observable artifacts (including structures and institutions of a culture)	Religion Type of government Mass communication (policy explanation)	Language barriers in coalition Planning Social rules governing house-to-house searches	Langauge barriers Religious norms Gender/age roles and rules Social norms (shaking hands, personal space) In-group/out-group Relationships/constraints Family structure Interpersonal communications
Values The base judgments of good and bad common to a culture	Trust formation Risk tolerance in uncertainty among coalition partners Risk tolerance in uncertainty of slow reconstruction effort Consensus-building in coalition	Speed of decisionmaking Focus of decisionmaking in organization (command authority) Risk tolerance in uncertainty Trust formation Perception in risk situations Distribution of authority in targets Understanding PSYOP Communication	Speed of decisionmaking Consensus building Risk tolerance in uncertainty Response to threats Trust formation Perception of risk in situations Negotiation dynamic Reciprocation of acts Face saving
Cognition The preference based strategies used in decisionmaking, perception, and knowledge representation	Negotiation, argumentative styles; use of evidence and hypothetical reasoning to justify policy decisions	Perception of consequences Negotiation styles Argumentation styles Causal attribution	Perception of consequences Negotiation styles Augmentation styles Causal attribution

Figure 14. Implications of culture at the strategic, operational, and tactical levels of war.

and wage country- (and even area-) specific information campaigns to support US themes and messages and de-legitimize extremism and terrorism.[56]

The cultural awareness model should be applied across the full spectrum of operations. Figure 14 represents a snapshot of how this model can be applied across the spectrum of the strategic, operational, and tactical levels of war. It is an example of how to think of culture and its manifestation at the strategic, operational, and tactical levels.[57]

Using this model can help prevent "information fratricide" against the United States' own objectives. This model can also assist commanders and staffs in defining the sphere of influence (SOI) within a designated AOR. The SOI defines ownership and responsibility. An SOI is a nondoctrinal informational term that represents a fixed relationship between military leaders and a target audience. Understanding SOIs can reduce "information fratricide." Information fratricide results from employing information operations elements in a way that adversely affects friendly operations or forces in the information environment.[58] By referencing this model, the US military can ensure that its themes and messages are congruent both vertically and horizontally. Furthermore, using this model ensures that the interagency is tied in and everyone is working toward the same ends.

Conclusion

The recommendations discussed in this chapter are designed to ensure that military planners are aware of and consider culture and religion throughout the CES process. Although cultural awareness is not the "be all and end all" of military planning, a thorough consideration of cultural factors will allow military planners to better identify and develop options for mitigating risk and avoid unintended problems associated with cultural ignorance. The kinds of recommendations discussed in this chapter, as well as the cultural awareness model as a whole, can help support improved planning and decision-making in both future combat and postconflict stability operations and ensure information operations consistency and congruency. Incorporating cultural awareness into training and doctrine is critical to such improvements.

Notes

1.   Ben Connable and Art Speyer, "Cultural Awareness for Military Operations," *Concepts and Proposals: USMC Cultural Awareness Working Group* (HQMC and MCIA, February 2005).

2.   Figure 9 was developed by Connable and Speyer (2005).

3.   University of Colorado International Online Training Program on Intractable Conflict, "Conflict Management and Constructive Confrontation: A Guide to the Theory and Practice," online at <http://www.colorado.edu/conflict/peace/index.html> (as of 24 August 2005).

4.   Connable and Speyer (2005).

5.   Glen Fisher, *International Negotiation: A Cross-Cultural Perspective* (Yarmouth, ME: Intercultural Press, Inc., 1980), 192.

6.   The term "three-block war" was coined by General Charles Krulack, Commandant of the Marine Corps from 1995–99.

7.   This is recognized in the 1994 version of Army Field Manual 100-23, *Peace Operations*, which states, "population distribution, ethnic backgrounds, languages, religious beliefs, and political loyalties of civilian personnel all emerge as significant components of successful intelligence collection." Headquarters, Department of the Army, FM 100-23, *Peace Operations* (Washington, DC: Headquarters, Department of the Army, 30 December 1994), 46.

8.   Adapted from Connable and Speyer (2005).

9.   Center for Army Lessons Learned (CALL), "Chapter 2: Civil Military Operations—Civil Affairs, Topic C: Cultural Issues in Iraq," in *Operation Iraqi Freedom (OIF)*, CAAT II Initial Impressions Report (IIR) No. 04-13 (Fort Leavenworth, KS: Center for Army Lessons Learned, May 2004). Online at <http://www.globalsecurity.org/military/library/report/call/call_04-13_chap01-c.htm> (as of 28 February 2006), 1.

10.   Ibid.

11.   Alvin and Heidi Toffler, *War and Anti-War: Survival at the Dawn of the Twenty-First Century* (Boston, MA: Little Brown and Company, 1993), 74.

12.   LTC Mark Corda, Commander, 3d Squadron, 2d Armored Cavalry Regiment, Bosnia and Herzegovina.

13.   Robert H. Scales, Jr., "Culture-Centric Warfare," *Proceedings*, September 2004.

14.   MG Paul Eaton, "Cultural Training in Professional Military Education (PME) Courses Policy Guidance," Memorandum for Commander, US Army Combined Arms Center and Fort Leavenworth.

15.   Ibid.

16.   Ibid.

17.   DOD Directive 1315.17 [Service Foreign Area Officer (FAO) Programs], dated 22 February 1997, directs all services to have FAO programs and specifies the prerequisite skills required of FAOs: regionally focused

graduate-level education; professional-level foreign language skills; and qualification in a principal military specialty. Implementation varies significantly among the services. Generally, Army officers apply for the FAO program as captains with five to six years of service (YOS). After company-level command, officers begin training at eight to ten YOS. Each officer learns a foreign language, conducts extended in-country training (ICT), and earns a regionally focused graduate degree. The Army's Career Field Designation (CFD) Board formally selects FAOs at their tenth YOS (as majors), after which they serve the remainder of their careers in FAO assignments.

18. Scales (2004).

19. DOD Directive 1315.17 (2005), 2.

20. Ibid.

21. Deputy Secretary of Defense Paul Wolfowitz, "Foreign Area Officer Programs," Memorandum, 28 April 2005.

22. Joint Chiefs of Staff, Joint Publication 1-02, *Department of Defense Dictionary of Military and Associated Terms*, 12 April 2001 (as amended through 31 August 2005), online at <http://131.84.1.34/doctrine/jel/doddict/> (as of 2 March 2006).

23. CALL (2004).

24. Headquarters, Department of the Army, FM 1, *The Army* (Washington, DC: Department of the Army, June 2005), 1–19.

25. The author was asked to provide input and help revise future versions of FM 3-0, *Operations*; FM 5-0, *Army Planning and Orders Production*, and FM 3-07.22, *Counterinsurgency.*

26. John Strycula, "Assessing Information Operations in Operation Iraqi Freedom (OIF): Interim Progress Report," to LTG(P) Wallace, Commander, Combined Arms Center, Fort Leavenworth, KS, 19 April 2005.

27. Headquarters, Department of the Army, FM 7-15, *Army Universal Task List* (Washington, DC: Department of the Army, August 2003).

28. Headquarters, Department of the Army, FM 2-0, *Intelligence* (Washington, DC: Department of the Army, May 2004), 1–38.

29. LTC John Strycula served in Iraq for twelve months with the 4th Infantry Division as the deputy G2. Since December 2003, the author has traveled monthly to the Joint Readiness Training Center, Fort Leavenworth, and other Army installations to teach Cultural Awareness to senior military leaders and nearly every Brigade Combat Team that has deployed to Iraq over the last twenty-four months. As a Middle East FAO, he conducted cultural awareness training at Fort Campbell, Fort Drum, Fort Hood, Fort Meade, the Defense Language Institute, and lectured at the FA 30 Information Operations Course at Fort Leavenworth, Kansas. Furthermore, he presented his brief entitled "Through the Lens of Cultural Awareness: Planning Requirements for Wielding the Instruments of National Power" as part of RAND's Warfighting Seminar Series in November 2004 and has served as a Middle East cultural

consultant to the University of Southern California's Army-funded research center, the Institute for Creative Technologies.

30.   See FM 7-15 (2003), 1–30. The tasks listed in the figure are derived from Army Task (ART) 1.4.2, "Provide Intelligence Support to Information Operations," and are representative of the types of support intelligence is expected to perform in today's contemporary operating environment.

31.   3d Infantry Division, *OPERATION IRAQI FREEDOM After Action Report*, December 2003, 269.

32.   Gregory Fontenot, E. J. Dugan, and David Tohm, *On Point: The United States Army in Operation Iraqi Freedom* (Fort Leavenworth, KS: Combat Studies Institute Press, 2004), 419.

33.   The Intelligence Battlefield Operating System (IBOS) is described as "the activity to generate knowledge of and products portraying the enemy and environmental features required by a commander in planning, *preparing*, executing, and assessing operations (FM 7-15)." GlobalSecurity.org, *Military Glossary*, online at <www.globalsecurity.org/military/library/policy/army/fm/3-90/glossary.htm> (as of 2 March 2006).

34.   William D. Wunderle, "Through the Lens of Cultural Awareness: Planning Requirements in Wielding the Instruments of National Power," RAND Technology and Applied Sciences Group Seminar, *Warfighters Operational Realities*, 17 November 2004.

35.   In-progress review meeting with LTG William Wallace, Commanding General, Combined Arms Center, Fort Leavenworth, KS, 19 April 2005.

36.   LTC Michael L. Warsocki, Land Information Warfare Activity, *Intelligence Support to Information Operations*, 1 March 2005, 33.

37.   Strycula (2005).

38.   3d Infantry Division (2003), 69.

39.   82d Airborne Division, *Lessons Learned by the 82d Airborne Division During OPERATION IRAQI FREEDOM,* 1 May 2003, 22.

40.   Wunderle (2004).

41.   Adopted from Defense Advanced Research Projects Agency, "Urban Sunrise," Final Technical Report, Veridian/General Dynamics, February 2004.

42.   Robert H. Scales, Jr., "Human Intel vs. Technology: Cultural Knowledge Important in Iraq," *Washington Times*, 3 February 2005, 21.

43.   Headquarters, Department of the Army, FM 2-01.3, *Intelligence Preparation of the Battlefield* (Draft) (Washington, DC: Department of the Army, May 2004), 1–5.

44.   Training and Doctrine Command (TRADOC), *Contemporary Operating Environment*, White Paper, 2 February 2002, 4.

45.   Defense Advanced Research Project Agency (2004), 137.

46.   Warsocki (2005), 17.

47.   Arthur K. Cebrowski served as the Director, Force Transformation,

and reported directly to the Secretary and Deputy Secretary of Defense. In this role, Admiral Cebrowski was an advocate, focal point, and catalyst for all transformation activities related to the Department of Defense.

48.   David S. Alberts, John J. Garstka, Richard E. Hayes, and David A. Signori, *Understanding Information Age Warfare*, DOD Command and Control Research Program, August 2001, 12–14. Online at <http://www.dodccrp.org/publications/pdf/Alberts_UIAW.pdf> (as of 2 March 2006).

49.   Ibid., 13.

50.   Ibid., 12.

51.   Adopted from Defense Advanced Research Project Agency (2004), 22–23.

52.   Headquarters, Department of the Army (HQDA), "Appendix A: Urban Terrain Analysis," in FM 90–10, *Military Operations on Urbanized Terrain (MOUT)* (Washington, DC: Department of the Army, 15 August 1979).

53.   Steven D. Biddle, Andrew Krepinevich, and Robert Scales, "Testimony Before the House Committee on Armed Services on Operation Iraqi Freedom: Operations and Reconstruction," 21 October 2003.

54.   Calvin F. Swain, Jr., *The Operational Planning Factors of Culture and Religion*, Newport, RI: US Naval War College, 13 May 2003.

55.   Ibid., 2.

56.   Defense Science Board 2004 Summer Study, "Transition to and from Hostilities," September 2004, 22.

57.   Defense Advanced Research Project Agency (2004), 141–142.

58.   CALL (2004), 7.

Chapter 5

Summary and Conclusions

Lessons learned studies from Somalia, Afghanistan, and Iraq consistently point to a lack of cultural awareness as a major impediment to mission success. There is a growing awareness among America's national and military leadership of the need to include cultural awareness as part of military operations. Cultural awareness can reduce battlefield friction and the fog of war, and improve the ability of leaders and US soldiers to accomplish the mission by providing insight into the intent of actors and groups in the battlespace, thus allowing the military to outthink and outmaneuver them. Finally, cultural awareness reduces cultural friction and can help the United States build rapport and prevent misunderstandings that detract from mission accomplishment.

However, despite the inclusion of cultural awareness and cultural intelligence at the Combat Training Centers, the schoolhouses (Fort Huachuca and Fort Leavenworth, for example), and in some military doctrine, to date there has been little in the way of operational knowledge on how to use this information once an AOR has been analyzed through a cultural lens. There is description, but little prescription.

Chapter 2 discussed a model that can be used to help the US military "operationalize" cultural awareness and intelligence in ways that are relevant to both combat and postconflict support operations. The key features of the model are:

- Cultural influences: Major social or institutional factors, such as heritage, religion, traditions, and language that bind people together.
- Cultural variations: Styles of behavior values and ways of thinking that are common to a culture.
- Cultural manifestations: The concrete displays of a culture's thought and behavior, whether through its members' view of authority, negotiation style, willingness to compromise, embracing of risk, or other means.

This model was used to define key aspects of Middle Eastern culture, with specific examples from Iraq.

As described in chapter 4, the full benefit of the cultural awareness model can be realized only if cultural awareness is integrated into US military training and doctrine. Table 11 provides a summary of the recommendations made in chapter 4 regarding this integration.

The Way Ahead

While there are a number of ongoing initiatives to factor the role of culture and religion into operations planning and execution as well as military training

Table 11. Summary of Recommendations.

Area of Interest	Recommendation
Training	• Ensure that cultural awareness is formally integrated into the Professional Military Education (PME) and Noncommissioned Officer Education System (NCOES).
	• Expand the Foreign Area Officer (FAO) program to ensure that a sufficient number of military officers are trained in this area.
Doctrine	• Add a subparagraph to IPB doctrine specifically dedicated to the cultural intelligence factors and discuss their effects on both friendly and enemy operations.
	• Incorporate into the intelligence analysis of the enemy a discussion of the effects and impacts that an adversary's culture will have on their decisions and tactics.
	• Adapt the deliberative planning process to incorporate cultural intelligence.
	• To support strategic communications during the execution of military operations, distinguish among issues relevant to friendly, failing, and failed states.
	• Apply the cultural awareness model across the full spectrum of the strategic, operational, and tactical levels of war.

and doctrine, the military must ensure that the sole focus of these efforts is not Middle East-, Iraq-, or Afghanistan-specific. The cultural awareness program specified in this document can apply across cultures and regions worldwide. Although the immediate focus is on Iraq, other regions, including North Korea and Iran, should also be areas of cultural attention. The development and maintenance of cultural competencies is a continuous process, and military leaders need to always be looking ahead and looking to understand multiple cultures at one time.

Glossary

A.H.	Anno Hegirae (year of the Hijra)
AOR	area of responsibility
ART	Army Task
AUTL	Army Universal Task List
BBC	British Broadcasting Company
BC	Before Christ
BOS	battlefield operating system
C2	command and control
C4ISR	command, control, communications, computers, intelligence, surveillance, and reconnaissance
CA	Civil Affairs
CAC	Combined Arms Center
CALL	Center for Army Lessons Learned
CCIR	commander's critical information requirements
CD	counterdrug
CENTCOM	Central Command
CES	commander's estimate of the situation
CFD	Career Field Designation
CFLCC	Combined Force Land Component Commander
CG	Commanding General
CIA	Central Intelligence Agency
CJTF	Combined Joint Task Force
CJTF-7	Combined Joint Task Force-7
COA	course of action
COE	contemporary operating environment
COG	center of gravity
COIN	Counterinsurgency
CSS	combat service support
DA	Department of the Army
DARPA	Defense Advanced Research Project Agency
DC	District of Columbia
DIA	Defense Intelligence Agency
DISAM	Defense Institute of Security Assistance Management
DLI	Defense Language Institute
DLIFLC	Defense Language Institute Foreign Language Center
DOD	Department of Defense
DoS	Department of State
e.g.	for example
EBO	effects-based operations
EUCOM	European Command

FAO	Foreign Area Officer
FID	foreign internal defense
FM	field manual
G3	Assistant Chief of Staff, Operations and Plans
GWOT	Global War on Terrorism
HQDA	Headquarters, Department of the Army
HQMC	Headquarters, Marine Corps
HUMINT	Human Intelligence
i.e.	that is
IBOS	Intelligence Battlefield Operating System
ICT	in-country training
ID	identification
IIR	initial impressions report
IO	Information Operations
IOC	Information Operations Command
IPB	Intelligence Preparation of the Battlefield
J2	Intelligence, Joint Staff Directorate
JIPB	Joint Intelligence Preparation of the Battlefield
JP	Joint Publication
JRTC	Joint Readiness Training Center
JTF	Joint Task Force
KS	Kansas
LEA	law enforcement agencies
LNO	liaison officer
LTC	lieutenant colonel
LTG	lieutenant general
MA	Massachusetts
MCIA	Marine Corps Intelligence Agency
MCO	major combat operations
MDMP	military decisionmaking process
ME	Maine
MG	major general
MODA	Ministry of Defense and Aviation
MOOTW	military operations other than war
MOUT	military operations on urbanized terrain
MRX	Mission Rehearsal Exercise
MTT	Mobile Training Team
NATO	North Atlantic Treaty Organization
NCO	noncommissioned officer
NCOES	noncommissioned officer education system
NGO	nongovernmental organization
NSA	National Security Agency
NTC	National Training Center

OEF	Operation Enduring Freedom
OIF	Operation Iraqi Freedom
OPTEMPO	operation tempo
(P)	Promotable
PACOM	Pacific Command
PIR	priority intelligence requirements
PKO	peacekeeping operations
PME	Professional Military Education
PO	peace operations
PSYOP	psychological operations
RI	Rhode Island
ROE	rules of engagement
RPG	rocket propelled grenade
SASO	stability and support operations
SIGINT	Signals Intelligence
SOF	Special Operations Forces
SOI	sphere of influence
SSTR	Stability, Security, Transition, and Reconstruction
TRADOC	Training and Doctrine Command
UN	United Nations
UNOSOM	United Nations Operation in Somalia
UNSCR	United Nations Security Council Resolution
US	United States
USD(P&R)	Under Secretary of Defense for Personnel and Readiness
USMC	United States Marine Corps
vs.	versus
YOS	years of service

Bibliography

Articles and Testimony

Abell, Charles S. "Testimony Before the House Armed Services Committee Subcommittee on Total Force," United States House of Representatives, 24 March 2004.

Biddle, Steven D., Andrew Krepinevich, and Robert Scales. "Testimony Before the House Committee on Armed Services on Operation Iraqi Freedom: Operations and Reconstruction." 21 October 2003.

Buszynski, Leszek. "Negotiating Styles in the Middle East." *The Practising Manager*, vol. 13, no. 2 (1993): 19–21.

Cordesman, Anthony H. *US Strategic Interests in the Middle East and the Process of Regional Change.* Washington, DC: Center for Strategic and International Studies, 1 August 1996. Online. Available at http://www.csis.org/component/option,com_csis_pubs/task,view/id,1686/ (as of 2 March 2006).

Duffey, Tamara. "Cultural Issues in Contemporary Peacekeeping." *International Peacekeeping*, vol. 7, no. 1 (2000): 142–168.

Fallow, James. "The Hollow Army." *The Atlantic Monthly*, March 2004.

Florin, J. "A Cognitive Explanation for the Influence of Culture on Strategic Choice in International Business." Eastern Academy of Management Meeting, Washington, DC, 1996.

Franke, R. H., G. Hofstede, and M.H. Bond. "Cultural Roots of Economic Performance: A Research Note." *Strategic Management Journal*, vol. 12 (1991): 165–173.

Hofstede, Geert. "National Cultures Revisited." *Behavior Science Research,* vol. 18 (1983): 285–305.

Israel, Steve, and Robert Scales. "Iraq Proves It: Military Needs Better Intel." *New York Daily News*, 7 January 2004.

Johnson, Silas R., Jr. "United States Military Training Mission: A Paradigm for Regional Security." *The DISAM Journal*, Summer 2001.

Keeney, R. L. "Creativity in Decision Making with Value-Focused Thinking." *Sloan Management Review*, Summer 1994, 33–41.

LeBaron, Michelle. "Transforming Cultural Conflict in an Age of Complexity." Berghof Handbook for Conflict Transformation. Berghof Research Center for Constructive Conflict Management, April 2001.

Mitrovica, David. "International Negotiations." *CSEG Recorder*, March 2001, 48–50.

Ryan, P. M. "Sociolinguistic Goals for Foreign Language Teaching and Teachers' Metaphorical Images of Culture." *Foreign Language Annals*, vol. 29, no. 4 (1996).

Salacuse, Jeswald W. "Ten Ways That Culture Affects Negotiating Style: Some Survey Results." *Negotiation Journal* (July 1998): 221–240.

Scales, Robert H., Jr. "Army Transformation: Implications for the Future." Statement of Major General Robert Scales, USA (Ret.), testifying before the House Armed Services Committee on 14 July 2004.

———. "Culture-Centric Warfare." *Proceedings*, September 2004.

———. "Human Intel vs. Technology: Cultural Knowledge Important in Iraq." *Washington Times*, 3 February 2005.

Skelton, Ike, and Jim Cooper. "You're Not from Around Here, Are You?" *Joint Forces Quarterly*, vol. 36 (December 2004): 12–16. Online. Available at http://www.dtic.mil/doctrine/jel/jfq_pubs/0436.pdf (as of 28 February 2006).

Yandura, Matthew J. "Allies Train, Jump Together," *Soldiers Magazine*, October 2002. Online. Available at http:www4.army.mil/soldiers/archive/oct2002/pdfs/postmarks.pdf (as of 2 March 2006).

Books and Documents

Acuff, Frank L. *How to Negotiate with Anyone Anywhere Around the World*, new expanded ed. New York: AMACOM, 1997.

Ahmed, M.M. *International Marketing and Purchasing of Projects: Interactions and Paradoxes—A Study of Finnish Project Exports to the Arab Countries.* Helsingfors: Swedish School of Economics and Business Administration, 1993.

Alberts, David S., John J. Garstka, Richard E. Hayes, and David A. Signori. *Understanding Information Age Warfare.* DOD Command and Control Research Program, August 2001. Online. Available at http://www.dodccrp.org/publications/pdf/Alberts_UIAW.pdf (as of 2 March 2006).

Cassirer, Ernst. *An Essay on Man.* New Haven, CT: Yale University Press, 1944.

Cunningham, Robert B. and Yasin K. Sarayrah. *Wasta: The Hidden Force in Middle Eastern Society.* Westport, CT: Praeger, 1993.

Fisher, Glen. *International Negotiation: A Cross-Cultural Perspective.* Yarmouth, ME: Intercultural Press, Inc., 1980.

———. *Mindsets: The Role of Culture and Perception in International Relations*, 2d ed. Yarmouth, ME: Intercultural Press, Inc., 1997.

Fisher, Roger, and William Ury. *Getting to Yes: Negotiating Agreement Without Giving In.* New York: Penguin Books, 1983.

Hitti, P. *The Arabs: A Short History.* Washington DC: Regnery Gateway, 1985.

Hofstede, Geert. *Culture and Organizations: Software of the Mind*, 2d rev. New York: McGraw-Hill, 1997.

Karney, Benjamin, Marcia Ellison, Heather Gregg, Sabrina Pagano, William Wunderle, and Scott Gerwehr. *A Framework to Analyze Cross-Cultural Diversity for Intelligence Tradecraft.* Unpublished RAND Research, 2006.

Lawrence, T. E. *Seven Pillars of Wisdom.* New York: Penguin, 1962.

Lewis, Bernard. *The Crisis of Islam, Holy War and Unholy Terror.* Modern Library Edition. New York: Random House, Inc., 2003.

———. *The Middle East: A Brief History of the Last 2,000 Years.* New York: Scribner, 1995.

Medby, Jamison J., and Russell W. Glenn. *Street Smart: Intelligence Preparation of the Battlefield for Urban Operations.* Santa Monica, CA: The RAND Corporation, MR-1287-A, 2002.

Mehrabian, Albert. *Nonverbal Communication.* Chicago: Aldine-Atherton, 1972.

Metz, Helen Chapin. "Iraq: Historical Setting." Library of Congress Country Study, May 1988. Online. Available at http://historymedren.about.com/library/text/bltxtiraqmain.htm (as of 2 March 2006).

Nisbett, Richard E., and Ara Norenzayan, *Stevens' Handbook of Experimental Psychology*, 3d ed, edited by D. L. Medin. New York: John Wiley & Sons, Inc., 2002.

Nydell, Margaret K. (Omar). *Understanding Arabs: A Guide for Westerners*, 3d ed. Yarmouth, ME: Intercultural Press, Inc., 2002.

Patai, Raphael. *The Arab Mind.* Hatherleigh Press, May 2002.

Rana, Kishan S. "Bilateral Diplomacy," Bilateral Negotiation. DiploProject: Geneva and Malta, 2002.

Rumsfeld, Donald H. *The National Defense Strategy of the United States of America*, March 2005.

Smith, Max. "International Business Negotiations: A Comparison of Theory with the Perceived Reality of Australian Practitioners." School of Commerce. The Flinders University of South Australia. Research Paper Series: 00-9, ISSN: 1441-3906, undated. Online. Available at http://www.ssn.flinders.edu.au/commerce/researchpapers/00–9.doc (as of 2 March 2006).

Solberg, Carl Arthur. *Culture and Industrial Buyer Behavior: The Arab Experience.* Dijon, France, September 2002.

Toffler, Alvin, and Heidi Toffler. *War and Anti-War: Survival at the Dawn of the 21st Century.* Boston, MA: Little, Brown, and Company, 1993.

Touma, Habib Hassan. *The Music of the Arabs*, new expanded ed., trans. Laurie Schwartz. Portland, OR: Amadeus Press, 1996.

Triandis, H. C. *Culture and Social Behavior.* New York: McGraw-Hill, 1994.

Wehr, Hans. *A Dictionary of Modern Arabic*, 4th ed., edited by J. M. Cowan. Ithaca, NY: Spoken Language Services, 1994.

Whorf, Benjamin Lee. *Language, Thought and Reality.* Cambridge, MA: MIT Press, 1964.

Wilson, Jeremy. *Lawrence of Arabia: The Authorized Biography of T. E. Lawrence.* New York: Atheneum, 1989.

Military and Technical Reports and Presentations

1st US Army Information Operations Command. "Intelligence Support to IO." Undated briefing.

3d Infantry Division. *OPERATION IRAQI FREEDOM After Action Report.* December 2003.

82d Airborne Division. *Lessons Learned by the 82d Airborne Division During OPERATION IRAQI FREEDOM.* 1 May 2003.

Center for Army Lessons Learned (CALL), "Chapter 2: Civil Military Operations—Civil Affairs, Topic C: Cultural Issues in Iraq," in *Operation Iraqi Freedom (OIF).* Fort Leavenworth, KS: Center for Army Lessons Learned, CAAT II Initial Impressions Report (IIR) No. 04-13, May 2004. Online. Available at http://www.globalsecurity.org/military/library/report/call/call_04-13_chap02-c.htm (as of 28 February 2006).

CALL Handbook No. 04-14. *Effects Based Operations: Brigade to Company Level.* Fort Leavenworth, KS: Center for Army Lessons Learned, July 2004.

Connable, Ben and Art Speyer. "Cultural Awareness for Military Operations." *Concepts and Proposals: USMC Cultural Awareness Working Group.* HQMC and MCIA, February 2005.

Crumrine, Russell B. "The Middle East and North Africa: A Cultural Guide for Security Assistance Personnel." The Defense Institute of Security Assistance Management (DISAM), June 2000.

Defense Advanced Research Projects Agency. "Urban Sunrise," Final Technical Report. Veridian/General Dynamics, February 2004.

Defense Language Institute Foreign Language Center. *Dialog on Language Instruction.* Vol. 13, Nos. 1 and 2, edited by Lidia Woytak. Presidio of Monterey, 1999. Online. Available at http://www.dliflc.edu/academics/academic_materials/dli/DLIissues/DLI_v13.pdf (as of 23 February 2006).

Defense Science Board 2004 Summer Study. "Transition to and from Hostilities." September 2004.

Department of Defense. "Military Department Foreign Area Officer (FAO) Programs." Directive 1315.17. 28 April 2005.

Department of Defense. "Military Support for Stability, Security, Transition, and Reconstruction (SSTR) Operations." Directive Number 3000.05. 28 November 2005.

Eaton, Paul. "Cultural Training in Professional Military Education (PME) Courses Policy Guidance." Memorandum for Commander, US Army Combined Arms Center and Fort Leavenworth, Fort Leavenworth, KS.

Fontenot, Gregory, E. J. Dugan, and David Tohn. *On Point: The United States Army in Operation Iraqi Freedom.* Fort Leavenworth, KS: Combat Studies Institute Press, 2004.

Hall, E. T. *The Dance of Life: The Other Dimension of Time.* New York: Anchor Press, 1989.

Headquarters, Department of the Army (HQDA). FM 1, *The Army.* Washington, DC: Department of the Army, June 2005.

———. FM 2-0, *Intelligence.* Washington, DC: Department of the Army, May 2004.

————. FM 2-01.3 (Draft), *Intelligence Preparation of the Battlefield.* Washington, DC: Department of the Army, May 2004.

————. FM 3-0, *Operations.* Washington, DC: Department of the Army, June 2001.

————. FM 3.06-11, *Combined Arms Operations in Urban Terrain.* Washington, DC: Department of the Army, 2000.

————. FM 3-07, *Stability Operations and Support Operations.* Washington, DC: Department of the Army, February 2003.

————. FM 3-13, *Information Operations*, Washington, DC: Department of the Army, November 2003.

————. FM 3-90, *Tactics*, Washington, DC: Department of the Army, 4 July 2001.

————. FM 6-0, *Mission Command: Command and Control of Army Forces.* Washington, DC: Department of the Army, August 2003.

————. FM 7-15, *Army Universal Task List.* Washington, DC: Department of the Army, August 2003.

————. FM 27-100, *Legal Support to Operations.* Washington, DC: Department of the Army, 1 March 2000.

————. FM 34-1, *Intelligence and Electronic Warfare Operations.* Washington, DC: Department of the Army, 27 September 1994.

————. FM 34-36, *Special Operations Forces Intelligence and Electronic Warfare Operations.* Washington, DC: Department of the Army, 30 September 1991.

————. FM 34-130, *Intelligence Preparation of the Battlefield.* Washington, DC: Department of the Army, 8 July 1994.

————. FM 90-10, *Military Operations on Urbanized Terrain (MOUT).* Washington, DC: Department of the Army, 15 August 1979.

————. FM 100-5, *Operations.* Washington, DC: Department of the Army, 14 June 1993.

————. FM 100-23, *Peace Operations.* 30 December 1994.

Joint Chiefs of Staff. Joint Publication 1-02, *Department of Defense Dictionary of Military and Associated Terms*, 12 April 2001 (as amended through 31 August 2005). Online. Available at http://131.84.1.34/doctrine/jel/dod dict/ (as of 2 March 2006).

————. Joint Pub 3-07.3, *Joint Tactics, Techniques, and Procedures for Peace Operations*, 12 February 1999.

————. Joint Pub 5.00-1, *Joint Doctrine for Campaign Planning*, 25 January 2002.

Klein, Helen Altman, and Gary Klein. "Cultural Lens: Seeing Through the Eyes of the Adversary." Presented at the 9th CGF&BR Conference, 16–18 May 2000.

Land Information Warfare Activity, United States Army. Generic Intelligence Requirements for Information Operations, version 1.0, 31 May 2002.

Mohammed, Al Sallal [Lt Col, Jordanian Army]. "Cultural Awareness." Jordanian Army Peace Operations Training Center.

Sampson, Kenneth L. "Instilling Passion for Language: Strategies and Techniques," in *Dialog on Language Instruction*, vol. 13, nos. 1 and 2. Presidio of Monterey: Defense Language Institute Foreign Language Center, 1999.

Strycula, LTC John. "Assessing Information Operations in Operation Iraqi Freedom (OIF): Interim Progress Report," to LTG(P) Wallace, Commander, Combined Arms Center, Fort Leavenworth, KS, 19 April 2005.

Swain, Calvin F., Jr. *The Operational Planning Factors of Culture and Religion.* Newport, RI: US Naval War College, 13 May 2003.

Training and Doctrine Command (TRADOC). *Contemporary Operating Environment.* White Paper, 2 February 2002.

United States Army Intelligence Center and Fort Huachuca. "Intelligence Officer's Handbook: Operation Iraqi Freedom Lessons Learned."

Warsocki, Michael L., LTC. Land Information Warfare Activity, Intelligence and Security Command. *Intelligence Support to Information Operations*, 1 March 2005.

Wunderle, William D. "Through the Lens of Cultural Awareness: Planning Requirements in Wielding the Instruments of National Power." RAND Technology and Applied Sciences Group Seminar. *Warfighters: Operational Realities*, 17 November 2004.

Web Sites

Christian Science Monitor. *Iraq in Transition.* Online. Available at http://www.csmonitor.com/world/iraq.html (as of 23 February 2006).

CIA World Fact Book. Online. Available at www.cia.gov/publications.

Coffman, James. "Does the Arabic Language Encourage Radical Islam?" *Middle East Quarterly*, December 1995. Online. Available at http://www.meforum.org/pf.php?id=276 (as of 23 February 2006).

Emery, Norman. "Information Operations in Iraq." *Military Review*, May–June 2004. Online. Available at http://usacac.leavenworth.army.mil/cac/milreview/download/English/MayJun04/emery.pdf (as of 23 February 2006).

Emery, Norman, Donald G. Mowles, and Jason Werchan. "Fighting Terrorism and Insurgency: Shaping the Information Environment." *Military Review*, January–February 2005. Online. Available at http://usacac.leavenworth.army.mil/CAC/milreview/English/JanFeb05/index.asp.

Hofstede, Geert. "A Summary of My Ideas About National Cultural Differences." Online. Available at http://feweb.uvt.nl/center/hofstede/page3.htm (as of 23 February 2006).

Iraq Country Study. Online. Available at http://memory.loc.gov/frd/cs/iqtoc.

Latif, Leyla Abdul. Iraqi Minister of Labor and Social Affairs in a 4 October 2004 interview with IRINnews.org. UN Office for the Coordination of

Humanitarian Affairs. Online. Available at http://www.irinnews.org/ report.asp (as of 7 April 2005).

LeBaron, Michelle. "Culture-Based Negotiation Styles," July 2003. Online. Available at http://www.beyondintractability.org/essay/culture_negotiation/ (as of 2 March 2006).

McCallister, William S. "The Iraq Insurgency: Anatomy of a Tribal Rebellion." Online. Available at http://www.firstmonday.org/issues/issue10_3/ mac/ (as of 21 March 2004).

Middle East News & World Report. Introduction to the Arab World. Online. Available at http://www.middleeastnews.com/intoarab101.html (as of 29 March 2005).

Military Glossary, GlobalSecurity.org. Online. Available at www.globalsecurity. org/military/library/policy/army/fm/3-90/glossary.htm (as of 2 March 2006).

PBS Online News Hour. "The New Iraq." Online. Available at http://www.pbs. org/newshour/bb/middle_east/iraq/.

Pike, John. "Societal Framework." GlobalSecurity.org 2000–2005. Online. Available at http://www.globalsecurity.org/military/world/iraq/society. htm (as of 4 April 2005).

Salloum, Habeeb. "The Odyssey of the Arabic Language and Its Script." Online. Available at http://www.alhewar.com/habeeb_salloum_arabic_ language.htm (as of 19 February 2005).

University of Colorado International Online Training Program on Intractable Conflict. "Conflict Management and Constructive Confrontation: A Guide to the Theory and Practice." Online. Available at http://www. colorado. edu/conflict/peace/index.html (as of 24 August 2005).

University of Texas at Austin. Perry-Castañeda Library Map Collection: Iraq maps. Online. Available at http://www.lib.utexas.edu/maps/iraq.html (as of 23 February 2006).

Appendix A

Cultural Factors in US Joint and Army Doctrine

The military has used the term culture in many different ways over the last decade or so as more of its operations occur in highly populated regions.[1] Due to ongoing military operations in Iraq, Afghanistan, and other areas of responsibility (AORs), the terms "culture" and "cultural awareness" enjoy a wide use in today's military lexicon, yet is largely absent in military doctrine.

Culture in Military Operations

In an attempt to define the term "culture" as it relates to military operations, this appendix includes a survey of military documents over the past several years to give a sense of the varied uses of the term "culture" and the limitations of those uses. Culture has begun to receive some attention in military doctrine, often in the context of "cultural awareness." These terms, however, are not adequately defined or explained, resulting in a lack of precision and miscommunication with regard to their use.

A review of twenty-six joint publications (3,965 pages) and twenty-one Army field manuals (5,630 pages) found only 312 and 840 instances of the word "culture," respectively.[2] Additionally, military doctrine provides four conflicting definitions of culture and no definition of cultural awareness. The doctrinal definitions of culture are:

- JP 1-02, *Department of Defense Dictionary of Military and Associated Terms* (approved for both DOD and NATO): A feature of the terrain that has been constructed by man. Included are such items as roads, buildings, and canals; boundary lines; and, in a broad sense, all names and legends on a map.
- FM 3-05.301, *Psychological Operations Tactics, Techniques, and Procedures:* Culture is the set of shared meanings by which people understand their world and make sense of their own behavior and that of others (paragraphs D-13 and D-14).
- FMI 3-07.22, *Counterinsurgency Operations:* Culture is the ideology of a people or region and defines a people's way of life (paragraph D-12).
- FM 22-100, *Army Leadership:* Culture is a group's shared set of beliefs, values, and assumptions about what's important (paragraphs 2-42 and 2-59).

Finally, Merriam-Webster defines culture as "the integrated pattern of human knowledge, belief, and behavior that depends upon man's capacity for learning and transmitting knowledge to succeeding generations. . . . The customary beliefs, social forms, and material traits of a racial, religious, or social group. The set of shared attitudes, values, goals, and practices that characterizes a company or corporation." In these documents, culture often includes common elements such as beliefs, values, and religion, but also physical elements such as buildings and infrastructure.

Given this, chapter 2 defined culture as "a shared set of traditions, belief systems, and behaviors, shaped by many factors, including history, religion, ethnic identity, language, and nationality, that evolves in response to various pressures and influences and is learned through socialization; it is not inherent," while cultural awareness is defined as "the ability to recognize and understand the effects of culture on people's values and behaviors."

To convey a sense of the treatment of culture in military doctrine, what follows is a survey of military documents that mention or consider culture, cultural intelligence, or cultural awareness.

US Joint Doctrine

Joint Publication 2-01, *Joint and National Intelligence Support to Military Operations* (7 October 2004)—Includes mention of cultural differences among coalition partners in the J2 quick reaction checklist included in its appendix.

Joint Publication 2-01.3, *Joint Tactics, Techniques and Procedures for Joint Intelligence Preparation of the Battlespace* (24 May 2000)—Acknowledges that the human dimension considered in IO and PSYOP includes culture and that the JIPB analyst should avoid cultural bias in evaluating proposed COAs by considering the actions in context of the adversary's culture. Joint doctrine does caution that cultural differences among coalition partners can impact operations and those differences should be minimized. However, there is little mention of what a cultural assessment is, who is responsible for it, or how to capture cultural awareness and competence during the campaign planning process.

Joint Publication 3.0, *Doctrine for Joint Operations* (10 September 2001)—States that cultural differences should be considered when conducting coalition operations. Additionally, cultural factors as an underlying factor for the war or conflict must be understood to determine the conditions necessary for termination. However, there is no specific mention on how to address cultural needs in terms of selecting or developing a course of action for the joint or coalition task force.

Joint Publication 3-07, *Joint Doctrine for Military Operations Other than War* (16 June 1995)—Indicates that cultural factors may be a source of threats during foreign internal defense (FID) operations. Also, cultural factors are again discussed during multinational operations as a potential source of conflict between coalition members. It is suggested to plan for additional liaison and advisory requirements.

Joint Publication 3-07.03, *Joint Tactics, Techniques, and Procedures for Peace Operations* (12 February 1999)—Recognizes that tactics such as PSYOPs and information operations require an understanding of the cognitive and cultural makeup of the target, rather than just location and defensive capabilities. To get a message across, the sender must know how the receiver is going to interpret the message and respond. Special Operations Forces (SOF) can play a significant role in peacekeeping operations (PKO) because of their unique capabilities, training, and experience. SOF often has detailed regional knowledge of cultures and languages, as well as experience working with indigenous forces. SOF capabilities of PSYOP and CA are particularly important in peace operations (PO) for their understanding of the complexity of operating in cross-cultural environments.

Joint Publication 3-16, *Joint Doctrine for Multinational Operations* (5 April 2000)—Recognizes that cultural differences among coalition partners can influence the effectiveness of the operation. However, JP 3-16 takes things one step further and has three items on the Commander's Checklist for Multinational Operations that require assessing cultural differences and their impact on the coalition.

Joint Publication 5-00.1, *Joint Doctrine for Campaign Planning* (25 January 2002)—Mentions cultural intelligence as part of the IPB process. From a procedural perspective, the analysis of the adversary's centers of gravity is a key step in the joint intelligence preparation of the battlespace. In the third and four steps in the JIPB process, joint force intelligence analysts identify the adversary's COG. Conduct the analysis after an understanding of the broad operational environment has been obtained and before a detailed study of the adversary's forces occurs. The analysis addresses the adversary's leadership, fielded forces, resources, infrastructure, population, transportation systems, and internal and external relationships.

Joint Publication 5-00.2, *Joint Task Force (JTF) Planning Guidance and Procedures* (13 January 1999)—This is the only joint publication that specifically mentions the critical importance of understanding the enemy's culture. The JTF chaplain is tasked with providing an assessment to CJTF and staff on the cultural and religious influences on mission accomplishment. JP 5-00.2 states that understanding the enemy's and coalition forces cultures are vital in improving operational effectiveness and preventing misunderstandings. Additionally, in military operations other than war (MOOTW) it is important to understand the differences among the affected population's culture and that of the coalition force. Intelligence for MOOTW should address the critical importance of culture and should be used to gauge the potential reactions of the local population in their assessments. The JTF should form a combined intelligence center and exchange liaison personnel to eliminate potential problems between coalition partners concerning language, doctrine, and operational intelligence requirements. Joint intelligence doctrine makes little mention of the importance of cultural factors.

US Army Doctrine

FM 3-06.11, *Combined Arms Operations in Urban Terrain* (2000)—In this document, culture is defined as "the social fabric of a city," and includes cultural norms (food, sleep patterns, casual and close relationships, manners, and cleanliness), religious beliefs, and local government. (This may include nepotism, favor-trading, subtle sabotage, and indifference. While corruption is sometimes pervasive and institutionalized, the power of officials is primarily based on family connections, personal power base, and age, and only after that on education, training, and competence.)

FM 100-5, *Operations* (14 June 1993)—Recognizes that "each partner in combined operations possesses a unique cultural identity, the result of language, values, religious systems, and economic and social outlooks. Nations with similar cultures are more likely to have similar aspirations. Further, their armed forces will face fewer obstacles to interoperability in a combined force structure. Nations with divergent cultural outlooks have to overcome greater obstacles in a coalition or alliance. Armies reflect the national cultures that influence the way they operate. Sources of national pride and cultural sensitivities will vary widely, yet the combined force commander must accommodate them. Differences in work ethic, standards of living, religion, and discipline affect the way nations approach war. Commanders cannot ignore these differences because they represent potential major problems. Even seemingly minor differences, such as dietary restrictions or officer-soldier relationships, can have a great impact. Commanders may have to accommodate religious holidays, prayer calls, and other unique cultural traditions that are important to allies" (page 5-2).

FM 100-23, *Peace Operations* (30 December 1994)—Describes conducting an analysis of the local area, which includes, "ethnic backgrounds, languages, and religious beliefs; tribe, clan, and subclan loyalties . . . holiday and religious observances practiced by the local populace" (page 46). The manual goes on to say, "All personnel involved in peace operations must receive training on the customs of the local population and coalition partners" (page 88), but provides no guidance on how to accomplish this.

FM 34-130, *Intelligence Preparation of the Battlefield* (8 July 1994)—Discusses the concept of conducting an IPB for operations other than war. The rest of the document considers friendly forces and threats, but no one else. The sections on Humanitarian Assistance and Peacekeeping Operations and

Peace Enforcement deal with some aspects of cultural intelligence (though not named as such). These cultural aspects include:

- Population distribution patterns.
- Ethnic divisions.
- Religious beliefs.
- Language divisions.
- Tribe, clan, and subclan loyalties.
- Political sympathies.
- Demographics:
  - ➤ Roots of conflict.
  - ➤ Belligerents.
  - ➤ Trust.
- Outside influence: organizations and media.

FM 34-36, *Special Operations Forces Intelligence and Electronic Warfare Operations* (30 September 1991)—Discusses the concepts described in this manuscript, although it does not use the same terminology relevant to the discussion of cultural intelligence. In addition to the normal structural and infrastructural aspects of the area of interest, the battle area evaluation for Special Operations Forces includes:

- Political.
- Military.
- Economic.
- Social.
- Geographic.
- Psychological.
- Cultural.
- Friendly forces.
- Hostile forces.
- Nonbelligerent.
- Third-party forces.

For psychological operations, the battle area evaluation includes other cultural features:

- Ethnic, racial, social, economic, religious, linguistic groups: locations and densities.
- Stances of groups: progovernment, neutral, proinsurgent.
- Key leaders and communicators: politicians/government and business/ clergy.
- Cohesive and divisive issues within.
- Community (e.g., attitudes toward United States).
- Literacy rates, education levels.

- Types and proportions of media.
- Consumed by community.
- Concentrations of third-country nationals in area: purpose and function.

Additionally, some of this information is represented as part of a Population Status Overlay on a map that includes the information above, and may include home and work places of key players and their relatives.

FM 27-100, *Legal Support to Operations* (1 March 2000)—Describes the complexity of MOOTW missions because of their impact on civilians. It states that "Commanders must be prepared to collect human intelligence concerning political, cultural, and economic factors affecting the operation; to conduct public affairs, civil affairs, and psychological operations; to provide humanitarian assistance; to develop rules of engagement (ROE) that protect the force without causing civilian casualties; to process civilian detainees; to process requests for temporary refuge or asylum; and to perform other tasks as the mission requires."

FM 3-07, *Stability Operations and Support Operations* (20 February 2003)—This is the most complete and up-to-date doctrinal manual in terms of cultural awareness. This manual provides a wide-reaching view of culture and its importance in operations. In particular, it deals with cultural differences, intelligence gathering, liaison, and negotiation. Of note, culture is included in the IPB process as an artifact: "The information gathering should focus on areas that influence people, such as cultures, politics, religion, economics, and related factors and any variances in affected groups of people."[3] At other times, culture also has cognitive connotations: "Culture shapes how people reason, what they accept as fact, and what principles they apply to decisionmaking."[4] Additionally, this manual provides one of the best views of culture and its implications as follows:

Clash of Cultures

1-30. Some in the non-Western world reject Western political and cultural values. In some instances, regimes that use Western political forms of government are under attack by ethnic, religious, and nationalist groups seeking to establish or reestablish their identity. As tribal, nationalist, or religious movements compete with Western models of government, instability can increase. This instability threatens not only Western interests within the state, but often threatens to spill across borders.[5]

CROSS-CULTURAL INTERACTION

1-69. Interacting with other cultures can create a significant challenge during stability operations and support operations. Often, adjustments in attitudes or methods must be made to accommodate different cultures. Ethnocentrism and cultural arrogance can damage relationships with other forces, NGOs, or indigenous populations. The welfare and perceptions of indigenous populations are often central to the mission during stability operations and support operations. Army forces must establish good working relations with indigenous populations. Mutual trust and rapport increase the chances for mission success.

1-70. Army personnel should understand the culture and history of the area. Historical understanding helps soldiers comprehend the society, interact with the people in that society, and adapt to cultural differences to facilitate rather than impede mission accomplishment. Historical and cultural understanding help to determine the range of actions acceptable in solving the problem at hand. With this in mind, soldiers must receive cultural and historical orientations to the people and the conflict. Civil affairs units produce area studies that can provide this information. Interpreters, translators, and linguists are also invaluable.[6]

PRIORITY INTELLIGENCE REQUIREMENTS

2-14. Priority intelligence requirements (PIR) in stability operations and support operations may differ from those in offensive and defensive operations. In combat operations, PIR focuses on the enemy's military capability and intentions. However, intelligence collection in stability operations and support operations may adjust to the people and their cultures, politics, crime, religion, economics, and related factors, and any variances within affected groups of people.

2-15. Generally, in offensive and defensive operations, PIR are answered and targets are attacked and destroyed. In stability operations and support operations, collection and production to answer PIR may be ongoing tasks. For example, PIR related to treaty verification or force protection may continue as long as the mission requires."[7]

Intelligence Preparation of the Battlefield

4-83. Intelligence preparation of the battlefield (IPB) is a continuous process that includes gathering information on areas in which a unit might be required to operate. . . . It begins before deployment notification and may be based on open-source intelligence. When notification comes, having current information will reduce uncertainties regarding the adversaries, the environment—including the medical threat and terrain in a given area—and facilitate mission planning. Successful intelligence support during PO relies on continuous information collection and intelligence production.

4-84. Ground reconnaissance and meetings with key interagency, international organization, and NGO players are essential to IPB. The information gathering should focus on areas that influence people, such as cultures, politics, religion, economics, and related factors and any variances in affected groups of people.[8]

Intelligence, Planning, CSS, Training, and Manpower Support

5-36. Planning support can be one of the most effective means of support-ing the national CD effort. Army personnel support CD planning of both LEAs and host nations. Understanding the supported agency or host nation, its culture, and its people is critical. Planning support provided to LEAs must consider the organization's mission, current goals, structure or chain of command, measures of success, and even relationships with other gov-ernment agencies or countries. Planning support provided to host nations is similar to that provided to LEAs. However, the host nation's culture, historical perspectives, political climate, and economic conditions are considered.[9]

Liaison

A-87. The professional abilities of the LNO determine a successful liaison. Additional factors that contribute to successful liaisons are—

- Knowledge of the doctrine, capabilities, procedures, and culture of their organizations.
- Transportation.
- Language ability.
- Regional orientation.
- Communications.
- Single point of contact in the headquarters.
- In support of humanitarian assistance missions, functional skills, and experience aligning with the need for medical and logistics expertise.[10]

Be Attuned to Cultural Differences

E-6. Actions can have different connotations to members of other cultures. Culture shapes how people reason, what they accept as fact, and what princi-ples they apply to decisionmaking. Nonverbal behavior such as the symbolic rituals or protocols of the arrangement for a meeting also is important.

E-7. Negotiations can be conducted at several levels: negotiations among Unites States (US) agencies and departments; between multinational part-ners; between the military force and the United Nations (UN) agencies; and between the military and local leaders. In the joint, combined, and interagency environment, negotiations can be complex. Nonetheless, all negotiations require tact, diplomacy, honesty, patience, fairness, effective communica-tions, cross-cultural sensitivity, and careful planning.[11]

CONSIDER CULTURAL IMPLICATIONS

E-11. There are organizational cultures within the various agencies and departments of the US government as well as the international organizations that shape the context of negotiations. Equally important are national cultural differences. The negotiating team should include experienced interpreters. Their understanding of the cultural context of terms used is invaluable. Negotiators need more than literal translators.

E-12. Negotiation is only one means of resolving conflict. Negotiators should consider indigenous conflict resolution techniques in selecting their approach.[12]

Notes

1.   Defense Advanced Research Project Agency, "Urban Sunrise," Final Technical Report, Veridian/General Dynamic, February 2004.

2.   This research was conducted by Bill Lambert, Assistant Professor, Department of Joint and Multinational Operations, Command and General Staff College, Fort Leavenworth, KS.

3.   Headquarters, Department of the Army (HQDA), FM 3-07, *Stability Operations and Support Operations* (Washington, DC: Department of the Army, February 2003), 4-23.

4.   Ibid., E-1.

5.   Ibid., 1-10.

6.   Ibid., 1-18.

7.   Ibid., 2-4 and 2-5.

8.   Ibid., 4-22 and 4-23.

9.   Ibid., 5-9.

10.   Ibid., A-17.

11.   Ibid., E-1.

12.   Ibid., E-2.

Appendix B

The 27 Articles of T. E. Lawrence*

The following notes have been expressed in commandment form for greater clarity and to save words. They are, however, only my personal conclusions, arrived at gradually while I worked in the Hejaz and now put on paper as stalking horses for beginners in the Arab armies. They are meant to apply only to Bedu; townspeople or Syrians require totally different treatment. They are of course not suitable to any other person's need, or applicable unchanged in any particular situation. Handling Hejaz Arabs is an art, not a science, with exceptions and no obvious rules. At the same time we have a great chance there; the Sherif trusts us, and has given us the position (toward his Government) which the Germans wanted to win in Turkey. If we are tactful, we can at once retain his goodwill and carry out our job, but to succeed we have got to put into it all the interest and skill we possess.

1. Go easy for the first few weeks. A bad start is difficult to atone for, and the Arabs form their judgments on externals that we ignore. When you have reached the inner circle in a tribe, you can do as you please with yourself and them.

2. Learn all you can about your Ashraf and Bedu. Get to know their families, clans and tribes, friends and enemies, wells, hills and roads. Do all this by listening and by indirect inquiry. Do not ask questions. Get to speak their dialect of Arabic, not yours. Until you can understand their allusions, avoid getting deep into conversation or you will drop bricks. Be a little stiff at first.

3. In matters of business deal only with the commander of the army, column, or party in which you serve. Never give orders to anyone at all, and reserve your directions or advice for the C.O., however great the temptation (for efficiency's sake) of dealing with his underlings. Your place is advisory, and your advice is due to the commander alone. Let him see that this is your conception of your duty, and that his is to be the sole executive of your joint plans.

4. Win and keep the confidence of your leader. Strengthen his prestige at your expense before others when you can. Never refuse or quash schemes he may put forward; but ensure that they are put forward in the first instance privately to you. Always approve them, and after praise modify them insensibly,

---

*T. E. Lawrence, "The 27 Articles of T. E. Lawrence," *The Arab Bulletin* (Cairo), vol. 60, 20 August 1917, 348, in Jeremy Wilson, *Lawrence of Arabia: The Authorized Biography of T. E. Lawrence*, New York: Atheneum, 1989, 960.

causing the suggestions to come from him, until they are in accord with your own opinion. When you attain this point, hold him to it, keep a tight grip of his ideas, and push them forward as firmly as possibly, but secretly, so that to one but himself (and he not too clearly) is aware of your pressure.

5.   Remain in touch with your leader as constantly and unobtrusively as you can. Live with him, that at meal times and at audiences you may be naturally with him in his tent. Formal visits to give advice are not as good as the constant dropping of ideas in casual talk. When stranger sheikhs come in for the first time to swear allegiance and offer service, clear out of the tent. If their first impression is of foreigners in the confidence of the Sherif, it will do the Arab cause much harm.

6.   Be shy of too close relations with the subordinates of the expedition. Continual intercourse with them will make it impossible for you to avoid going behind or beyond the instructions that the Arab C.O. has given them on your advice, and in so disclosing the weakness of his position you altogether destroy your own.

7.   Treat the sub-chiefs of your force quite easily and lightly. In this way you hold yourself above their level. Treat the leader, if a Sherif, with respect. He will return your manner and you and he will then be alike, and above the rest. Precedence is a serious matter among the Arabs, and you must attain it.

8.   Your ideal position is when you are present and not noticed. Do not be too intimate, too prominent, or too earnest. Avoid being identified too long or too often with any tribal sheikh, even if C.O. of the expedition. To do your work you must be above jealousies, and you lose prestige if you are associated with a tribe or clan, and its inevitable feuds. Sherifs are above all blood-feuds and local rivalries, and form the only principle of unity among the Arabs. Let your name therefore be coupled always with a Sherif's, and share his attitude toward the tribes. When the moment comes for action put yourself publicly under his orders. The Bedu will then follow suit.

9.   Magnify and develop the growing conception of the Sherifs as the natural aristocracy of the Arabs. Intertribal jealousies make it impossible for any sheikh to attain a commanding position, and the only hope of union in nomad Arabs is that the Ashraf be universally acknowledged as the ruling class. Sherifs are half-townsmen, half-nomad, in manner and life, and have the instinct of command. Mere merit and money would be insufficient to obtain such recognition; but the Arab reverence for pedigree and the Prophet gives hope for the ultimate success of the Ashraf.

10.   Call your Sherif "Sidi" in public and in private. Call other people by their ordinary names, without title. In intimate conversation call a Sheikh "Abu Annad," "Akhu Alia" or some similar by-name.

11.   The foreigner and Christian is not a popular person in Arabia. However friendly and informal the treatment of yourself may be, remember always that your foundations are very sandy ones. Wave a Sherif in front of you like

a banner and hide your own mind and person. If you succeed, you will have hundreds of miles of country and thousands of men under your orders, and for this it is worth bartering the outward show.

12. Cling tight to your sense of humor. You will need it every day. A dry irony is the most useful type, and repartee of a personal and not too broad character will double your influence with the chiefs. Reproof, if wrapped up in some smiling form, will carry further and last longer than the most violent speech. The power of mimicry or parody is valuable, but use it sparingly, for wit is more dignified than humor. Do not cause a laugh at a Sherif except among Sherifs.

13. Never lay hands on an Arab; you degrade yourself. You may think the resultant obvious increase of outward respect a gain to you, but what you have really done is to build a wall between you and their inner selves. It is difficult to keep quiet when everything is being done wrong, but the less you lose your temper the greater your advantage. Also then you will not go mad yourself.

14. While very difficult to drive, the Bedu are easy to lead, if: have the patience to bear with them. The less apparent your interferences the more your influence. They are willing to follow your advice and do what you wish, but they do not mean you or anyone else to be aware of that. It is only after the end of all annoyances that you find at bottom their real fund of goodwill.

15. Do not try to do too much with your own hands. Better the Arabs do it tolerably than that you do it perfectly. It is their war, and you are to help them, not to win it for them. Actually, also, under the very odd conditions of Arabia, your practical work will not be as good as, perhaps, you think it is.

16. If you can, without being too lavish, forestall presents to yourself. A well-placed gift is often most effective in winning over a suspicious sheikh. Never receive a present without giving a liberal return, but you may delay this return (while letting its ultimate certainty be known) if you require a particular service from the giver. Do not let them ask you for things, since their greed will then make them look upon you only as a cow to milk.

17. Wear an Arab headcloth when with a tribe. Bedu have a malignant prejudice against the hat, and believe that our persistence in wearing it (due probably to British obstinacy of dictation) is founded on some immoral or irreligious principle. A thick headcloth forms a good protection against the sun, and if you wear a hat your best Arab friends will be ashamed of you in public.

18. Disguise is not advisable. Except in special areas, let it be clearly known that you are a British officer and a Christian. At the same time, if you can wear Arab kit when with the tribes, you will acquire their trust and intimacy to a degree impossible in uniform. It is, however, dangerous and difficult. They make no special allowances for you when you dress like them. Breaches of etiquette not charged against a foreigner are not condoned to you in Arab clothes. You will be like an actor in a foreign theatre, playing a part

day and night for months, without rest, and for an anxious stake. Complete success, which is when the Arabs forget your strangeness and speak naturally before you, counting you as one of themselves, is perhaps only attainable in character: while half-success (all that most of us will strive for; the other costs too much) is easier to win in British things, and you yourself will last longer, physically and mentally, in the comfort that they mean. Also then the Turks will not hang you, when you are caught.

19.   If you wear Arab things, wear the best. Clothes are significant among the tribes, and you must wear the appropriate, and appear at ease in them. Dress like a Sherif, if they agree to it.

20.   If you wear Arab things at all, go the whole way. Leave your English friends and customs on the coast, and fall back on Arab habits entirely. It is possible, starting thus level with them, for the European to beat the Arabs at their own game, for we have stronger motives for our action, and put more heart into it than they. If you can surpass them, you have taken an immense stride toward complete success, but the strain of living and thinking in a foreign and half-understood language, the savage food, strange clothes, and stranger ways, with the complete loss of privacy and quiet, and the impossibility of ever relaxing your watchful imitation of the others for months on end, provide such an added stress to the ordinary difficulties of dealing with the Bedu, the climate, and the Turks, that this road should not be chosen without serious thought.

21.   Religious discussions will be frequent. Say what you like about your own side, and avoid criticism of theirs, unless you know that the point is external, when you may score heavily by proving it so. With the Bedu, Islam is so all-pervading an element that there is little religiosity, little fervour, and no regard for externals. Do not think from their conduct that they are careless. Their conviction of the truth of their faith, and its share in every act and thought and principle of their daily life is so intimate and intense as to be unconscious, unless roused by opposition. Their religion is as much a part of nature to them as is sleep or food.

22.   Do not try to trade on what you know of fighting. The Hejaz confounds ordinary tactics. Learn the Bedu principles of war as thoroughly and as quickly as you can, for till you know them your advice will be no good to the Sherif. Unnumbered generations of tribal raids have taught them more about some parts of the business than we will ever know. In familiar conditions they fight well, but strange events cause panic. Keep your unit small. Their raiding parties are usually from one hundred to two hundred men, and if you take a crowd they only get confused. Also their sheikhs, while admirable company commanders, are too "set" to learn to handle the equivalents of battalions or regiments. Don't attempt unusual things, unless they appeal to the sporting instinct Bedu have so strongly, unless success is obvious. If the objective is a good one (booty) they will attack like fiends, they are splendid scouts, their mobility gives you the advantage that will win this local war, they make proper

use of their knowledge of the country (don't take tribesmen to places they do not know), and the gazelle-hunters, who form a proportion of the better men, are great shots at visible targets. A sheikh from one tribe cannot give orders to men from another; a Sherif is necessary to command a mixed tribal force. If there is plunder in prospect, and the odds are at all equal, you will win. Do not waste Bedu attacking trenches (they will not stand casualties) or in trying to defend a position, for they cannot sit still without slacking. The more unorthodox and Arab your proceedings, the more likely you are to have the Turks cold, for they lack initiative and expect you to. Don't play for safety.

23.   The open reason that Bedu give you for action or inaction may be true, but always there will be better reasons left for you to divine. You must find these inner reasons (they will be denied, but are none the less in operation) before shaping your arguments for one course or other. Allusion is more effective than logical exposition: they dislike concise expression. Their minds work just as ours do, but on different premises. There is nothing unreasonable, incomprehensible, or inscrutable in the Arab. Experience of them, and knowledge of their prejudices will enable you to foresee their attitude and possible course of action in nearly every case.

24.   Do not mix Bedu and Syrians, or trained men and tribesmen. You will get work out of neither, for they hate each other. I have never seen a successful combined operation, but many failures. In particular, ex-officers of the Turkish army, however Arab in feelings and blood and language, are hopeless with Bedu. They are narrow minded in tactics, unable to adjust themselves to irregular warfare, clumsy in Arab etiquette, swollen headed to the extent of being incapable of politeness to a tribesman for more than a few minutes, impatient, and, usually, helpless without their troops on the road and in action. Your orders (if you were unwise enough to give any) would be more readily obeyed by Beduins than those of any Mohammedan Syrian officer. Arab townsmen and Arab tribesmen regard each other mutually as poor relations, and poor relations are much more objectionable than poor strangers.

25.   In spite of ordinary Arab example, avoid too free talk about women. It is as difficult a subject as religion, and their standards are so unlike our own that a remark, harmless in English, may appear as unrestrained to them, as some of their statements would look to us, if translated literally.

26.   Be as careful of your servants as of yourself. If you want a sophisticated one you will probably have to take an Egyptian, or a Sudani, and unless you are very lucky he will undo on trek much of the good you so laboriously effect. Arabs will cook rice and make coffee for you, and leave you if required to do unmanly work like cleaning boots or washing. They are only really possible if you are in Arab kit. A slave brought up in the Hejaz is the best servant, but there are rules against British subjects owning them, so they have to be lent to you. In any case, take with you an Ageyli or two when you go up country. They are the most efficient couriers in Arabia, and understand camels.

27.   The beginning and ending of the secret of handling Arabs is unremitting study of them. Keep always on your guard; never say an unnecessary thing: watch yourself and your companions all the time: hear all that passes, search out what is going on beneath the surface, read their characters, discover their tastes and their weaknesses and keep everything you find out to yourself. Bury yourself in Arab circles, have no interests and no ideas except the work in hand, so that your brain is saturated with one thing only, and you realize your part deeply enough to avoid the little slips that would counteract the painful work of weeks. Your success will be proportioned to the amount of mental effort you devote to it.

Appendix C

Preparing for Negotiations in the Middle East

Historically, the negotiation of bilateral and multilateral agreements was one of the more important external relation tasks of governments. In fact, negotiating is regarded as the central function of diplomacy. However, because of increased OPTEMPO due to the Global War on Terrorism, Operation Enduring Freedom, Operation Iraqi Freedom, and other ongoing operations, the US Army now regularly participates in military operations, peacekeeping missions, and other ad hoc international actions that are fraught with cultural conflict potential—not only between foreign military personnel and local populations, but also between nationalities within the foreign forces.

One of the considerations that have arisen from this is the need to understand that the values of people from other organizations and nationalities will directly affect their understanding of any given situation. Recent experiences demonstrate that it has become commonplace during civil-military operations (as well as combat operations) for soldiers of all ranks to be involved with some sort of negotiation, dispute resolution, or bargaining for individual or collective advantages. This is particularly true in sudden, unexpected confrontational situations where action must be immediate and without prior preparation. Because of this, the success of military operations call for soldiers and leaders to exhibit expert cultural awareness and management skills in their day-to-day interactions and negotiations with persons from other cultures.

The term "negotiation" presupposes common interests and issues of conflict between the two sides. The object of bilateral negotiations is to resolve an issue that cannot be solved unilaterally through one's own actions. Engagement in a negotiation also implies a willingness to achieve a compromise somewhere between one's own maximum goal and the absolute minimum that one is willing to accept. The process involves the exchange of promises, assurances, and compromise. A negotiation becomes cross-cultural when the parties belong to different cultures and, therefore, do not share the same ways of thinking, feeling, and behaving.[1] With this definition as the premise, it can be argued that in today's US military operations overseas, military leaders from squad leader to flag officer will be required to conduct bilateral negotiations. During the conduct of bilateral negotiations, a balance has to be found between a short-term gain and establishing a long-term relationship to facilitate future interactions.[2] Furthermore, it is important to understand that bilateral negotiations conducted during the course of military operations with local national authorities are often complicated by the invisible presence of other stakeholders at the table. Done correctly, the conclusion of successful negotiations will further enhance a unit's ability to achieve its campaign goals, save lives, and facilitate the transition to a safe and secure environment.

The process of conducting bilateral negotiations involves a three-stage process: the prenegotiation stage, the negotiation, and, finally, the follow-up or postnegotiation stage. The prenegotiation phase of a bilateral negotiation is often the most critical. Each party identifies its strengths, assesses its interests, and works to understand the wider context of the negotiations. This is the phase in which it is important for a military leader to understand the cultural context in which his counterpart operates. Effective negotiators base their strategy and tactics on the characteristics of the situation and the people involved. A detailed course of instruction on how to conduct bilateral negotiations is beyond the scope of this study.[3] However, analyzing cultural differences as they relate to negotiation is not.

The analytical framework provided earlier is useful in preparing for the conduct of bilateral negotiations. Again, it must be emphasized that there is no one right approach to negotiations. There are only more effective and less effective approaches and these vary according to many contextual factors. As negotiators understand that their counterparts may see things very differently than themselves, they will be less likely to make negative judgments and more likely to make progress in negotiations.[4]

Countries vary on such key aspects as the amount and type of preparation for a negotiation, the relative time on task versus interpersonal relationships, the use of general principles versus specific details, and the number of people present and the extent of their influence. Although cultural stereotypes are simplistic, many of them contain elements of truth. For example, the United States is likely to give one negotiator complete control while negotiations with Middle Eastern cultures can be drawn out and contain many subtleties.[5] As such, we will look at how Arab and Middle Eastern cultural variations manifest themselves in the conduct of bilateral negotiations.[6]

In an article entitled "Ten Ways That Culture Affects Negotiating Style: Some Survey Results," Jeswald Salacuse outlined ten factors in the negotiation process that seem to be influenced by a person's culture.[7] He further proposed that the culturally different responses would fall on a point on a continuum between two polar extremes. Salacuse's ten factors and associated ranges of cultural responses are shown in table 12.[8]

Negotiating Goals: Contract or Relationship—Relates to the purpose or intent of the parties to the negotiation. In general, for American business negotiators the signing of a contract is their primary negotiating aim. They consider such a contract a binding agreement that outlines the roles, rights, and obligations of each party. In contrast, negotiators from Middle Eastern cultures are believed to have a more fluid view of contracts and, therefore, place more emphasis on establishing a sustainable business relationship rather than a contract. Furthermore, Middle Eastern cultures eschew the "Western tradition of legalism" and "prefer to leave things vague."[9] The importance of relationships when negotiating with most Middle East cultural groups cannot be

Table 12. The Impact of Culture on Negotiation.

Negotiation Factors	Range of Cultural Responses
Goal	Contract ←→ Relationship
Attitude	Win/Lose ←→ Win/Win
Personal Styles	Informal ←→ Formal
Communications	Direct ←→ Indirect
Time Sensitivity	High ←→ Low
Emotionalism	High ←→ Low
Agreement Form	Specific ←→ General
Agreement Building	Bottom Up ←→ Top Down
Team Organization	One Leader ←→ Consensus
Risk Taking	High ←→ Low

underestimated. Personal relationships are founded on loyalty and reciprocity and trust between the partners is never feigned.

Attitude: Win/Lose or Win/Win—This is also known as distributive or integrative bargaining, respectively. With distributive bargaining, the parties to the negotiation see each other's goals as incompatible and, therefore, believe one party can only gain at the expense of the other. With integrative bargaining, the parties to the negotiation consider themselves to have compatible goals and, therefore, assume both parties should stand to gain from the final agreement. All parties to a negotiation, regardless of cultural background, would prefer to come out ahead of the other party in business negotiations and the approach they bring to the negotiations is a factor of either their personality or their relative position of power.[10]

Personal Style: Formal or Informal—Relates to how negotiators interact with counterparts at the table. In the Middle East, while negotiators will generally insist on addressing counterparts by their titles, they tend to like longer, less formal sessions and are given to expressing philosophical statements. It is important for American negotiators to pay attention to these statements as they are often more important to the negotiation process than the technical issues of the problem.

As discussed earlier, Middle Eastern cultures are more tactile and allow more touching than Americans are used to. Greeting rituals fit with these patterns, so awareness of local norms is important for negotiators. Space also relates to comfort with eye contact and attributions related to eye contact or lack of eye contact. In Arab cultures, eye contact is a sign of reliability and trustworthiness. Closely related to notions of space is nonverbal communication. Arab culture is high context. Therefore, Arab negotiators attach great importance to context (history for example) and "make a sharp distinction between the way matters of state should be conducted and matters of commerce."[11] When communicating with Arabs, pay attention to body language, eye movements, and hand gestures. There are many dimensions of nonverbal communication that can be used to contradict, emphasize, or serve as a substitute for verbal messages.

Communications: Direct or Indirect—Relates to the literature's claims that people from certain cultures tend to adopt direct and simple methods of communication while people from other cultures tend to rely on indirect, more complex methods. Middle East cultures rely on high-context language and indirect communication. As such, an Arab negotiator's reaction to proposals may only be gained by interpreting seemingly indefinite comments, gestures, and nonverbal signs. Furthermore, most Middle Easterners are reluctant to say "no" directly. This relates to the issue of "face" and a preferred avoidance of conflict.

Time Sensitivity: High or Low—Relates to cultural differences in attitudes toward time and the length of time devoted to the negotiation itself. Americans view time as monochronic, sequential, absolute, and prompt. Middle Easterners view time as polychronic, nonlinear, repetitive, and associated with events. As such, Middle Eastern cultures tend to favor long negotiations and slow deliberations. The reason for this is that most Middle Eastern negotiators have a cultural preference to establish a relationship before they begin the negotiations proper; that is, they do not have a cultural preference for long negotiations—only for developing a relationship—and the consensus-based decision-making process of Arab and Middle Eastern culture.

Because of their orientation to time, Arab negotiations may involve simultaneous occurrences of many things and the involvement of many people. The time it takes to complete an interaction is elastic and more important than any schedule. Arabs tend to exchange pleasantries at some length before getting down to business. Likewise, Arabs use silent intervals for contemplation, whereas Americans seem to have little tolerance for silence during negotiations. Another dimension of time relevant to negotiations with Arabs is the focus on past. Negotiators focused on the present should be mindful that others might see the past as part of the present.[12]

Emotionalism: High or Low—Relates to the differing views between cultures as to the appropriateness of displaying emotions, as these differing cultural norms may be brought to the negotiating table. Again, as a high-context culture, Arab negotiators are more likely to show emotions at the negotiating table than American negotiators.

Form of Agreement: General or Specific—Relates to the culturally specific preference for the form of written agreement the contract takes. Americans prefer detailed contracts that attempt to anticipate all possible circumstances while Middle Easterners tend to prefer an agreement in the form of general principles rather than detailed rules. Instead of being fixed and unchangeable, an agreement in the Middle East is considered relatively flexible and is symbolic of the relationship that has been established rather than a legal document.

Building an Agreement: Bottom Up or Top Down—Relates to the culturally different processes for developing agreements. Middle East negotiators tend to begin negotiations by establishing general principles as the framework on which an agreement is built—a deductive or top-down process. Americans tend to begin negotiations by first dealing with the details—an inductive or bottom-up process.

Team Organization: One Leader or Group Consensus—Relates to the culturally specific ways different groups organize themselves and how decisions are made within the group. In the Middle East, while a negotiating team may have a designated leader who appears to have complete authority to decide all matters, a hidden authority rests with the group and decision-making often occurs through consensus. Therefore, negotiating teams may be relatively large because of the greater number of personnel involved in the decisionmaking process. This is closely related to the concept of power distance.

Power distance is used to describe the degree of deference and acceptance of unequal power between people. High power distance cultures are those where some people are considered superior to others because of their social status, gender, race, age, education, birth, personal achievements, family background, or other factors. Middle Eastern cultures are high power distance cultures and, therefore, are comfortable in high power distance situations. Because of this, Middle Eastern negotiators tend to be comfortable with hierarchical structures, clear authority figures, and using power with discretion, while at the same time remaining deferential to status.

Risk Taking: High or Low—Relates to research indicating certain cultures are more risk averse than others. Americans in general are the least risk averse; Middle Eastern culture is prone to avoiding uncertainty. Uncertainty avoidance has to do with the way national cultures relate to uncertainty and ambiguity, and how well they may adapt to change. This can affect their willingness to take risks in a negotiation—to divulge information, try new approaches, or tolerate uncertainties in a proposed course of action. Because of this, it may be difficult for outside negotiators to establish relationships of confidence and trust with members of these national cultures. Conversely, the United States has a higher tolerance for uncertainty, and, consequently, tends to value risk-taking, problem solving, flat organizational structures, and have a higher tolerance for ambiguity.[13]

The Concept of Face—It is important to reiterate the dual concepts of honor and shame in Arab and Middle Eastern cultures. "Face" refers to a person's reputation and the respect in which others hold him. Arab negotiators attach high importance to creating bonds of friendship and trust between negotiators and respect for the honor and dignity of negotiating partners. To an American, losing face may be embarrassing. To an Arab, losing face is devastating. It is the ultimate disgrace and he will go to almost any length to avoid a loss of face. The concept of face must be an important consideration in negotiations conducted in the Middle East.

The roles and uses of translators—The use of translators is an area meriting improvement. Due to a lack of trained military Arabic-speaking linguists and contracted third country translators, US forces are reliant on locally hired translators. This has the potential to cause problems due to the disproportionate influence and bias that translators tend to wield. This can result in some groups being favored at the expense of others, while the subsequent animosity toward the translator may be directed at American forces. In an extreme example of this, American forces that entered Iraq with Kuwaiti translators encountered a negative Iraqi response stemming from animosity between Iraqis and Kuwaitis. Similarly, tribal and sectarian affiliations of locally hired translators may interfere with US objectives and operations. In short, be aware of one's operating environment and the differences between the nationalities and ethnicities in the Middle East.[14]

Cultural Awareness: How Far to Adapt?

The question: How far to adapt? The answer: It depends. Cultural awareness is an art, not a science, and varies based on the circumstances and the parties involved. Some general guidelines, however, are appropriate.

First, not to cause serious offense, it is appropriate to show some degree of cultural sensitivity when carrying out cross-cultural negotiations. This is more than just avoiding culturally offensive actions—the do's and don'ts of typical cultural briefings. It also involves preserving face and demonstrating respect for one's counterpart. During a negotiation, the consequences of offending through cultural insensitivity can lead to impasses at best and nonnegotiated agreements (win/lose or lose/lose) at worst. Negotiations that fail because the negotiator was not willing to provide the level of respect considered appropriate by members of the other party cannot only lead to mission failure, but set any previous gains back for the unforeseeable future.[15]

Second, it is appropriate to "be oneself," but with respect to the culture of one's counterparts. It is not necessary or appropriate to be culturally subservient when conducting negotiations with members of a foreign culture. In fact, doing so may create a marked disadvantage. In other words, when in Rome, it may be appropriate to do as the Romans do; however, this does not mean that one should try to become Roman.[16] The rationale behind this contention, especially in the Middle East, is that one's counterpart wants to understand who you are and what type of person you are. As shown in figure 15, American negotiators are not generally perceived as being well prepared to conduct bilateral negotiations.[17]

Competency	Grade
• Preparation	B-
• **Synergistic approach (win/win)**	**D**
• **Cultural I.Q.**	**D**
• **Adapting the negotiating process to the host country environment**	**D**
• **Patience**	**D**
• **Listening**	**D**
• **Linguistic abilities**	**F**
• Using language that is simplistic and accessible	C
• High aspirations	B+
• Personal integrity	A-
• **Building solid relationships**	**D**

Figure 15. US negotiators' global report card.

These problems continue today as the US military attempts to deal with other cultures in the international arena. To be good negotiators, US military leaders must understand how Americans differ from others in terms of cultural traits, values, and assumptions. As a starting point, when communicating with people from another culture, use the following strategies:

- Show respect: Withhold judgment, accepting the premise that attitudes held by an entire culture are probably based on sound reasoning. Listen carefully to what is being communicated and try to understand your counterpart's feelings. Take the time to learn about the Middle East—its geography, its long history, its religion, etc. Try to speak the language. Truly knowing the language and culture involves far more than basic grammar and conversation skills. It is about credibility and building personal relationships. Knowing a foreign language can provide a personal and professional edge.
- Value diversity: A person who is knowledgeable about and comfortable with different cultures will be a more effective leader and negotiator because he can avoid misunderstandings and tap into the greater variety of viewpoints that Arabs can provide.

- Communicate Clearly: To ensure that your message is understood, follow these guidelines:
  - Avoid slang, jargon, military acronyms, and other figures of speech.
  - Be specific and illustrate your points with concrete examples.
  - Provide and solicit feedback. Summarize frequently, ask your counterpart to paraphrase what has been said and encourage questions.
  - Avoid attempts at humor. Jokes do not translate well and are likely to be lost on your counterpart.
  - Speak plainly and slowly—not so slowly as to appear condescending—and choose your words carefully.

As seen during the conduct of recent military operations, situations will arise in which military leaders will have to conduct some sort of negotiation, formal or informal, with a person or persons from another country. To be successful, military leaders at all levels must be sensitive to the cross-cultural dimensions of our unique operating environments. Traditionally, these issues have been largely ignored or not understood. The ability to conduct successful negotiations requires strong cross-cultural skills and is critical to winning the peace.

Notes

1.   David Mitrovica, "International Negotiations," *CSEG Recorder*, March 2001, 48–50.

2.   Kishan S. Rana, "Bilateral Diplomacy," Bilateral Negotiation, Diplo-Project: Geneva and Malta, 2002, 283. See also, Kristopher Blanchard, "Cross-Cultural Negotiation and Decision Making," PowerPoint briefing, North Central University, online as of 29 August 2005.

3.   An excellent primer for conducting negotiations is Roger Fisher and William Ury, *Getting to Yes: Negotiating Agreement Without Giving In*, New York: Penguin Books, 1983. In this text, Fisher and Ury describe their four principles for effective negotiation. They explain that a good agreement is one that is wise and efficient and that improves the parties' relationship. Wise agreements satisfy the parties' interests and are fair and lasting. The authors' goal is to develop a method for reaching good agreements. Negotiations often take the form of positional bargaining. In positional bargaining, each party opens with their position on an issue and the parties then bargain from their separate opening positions to agree on one position. Haggling over a price is a typical example of positional bargaining. Fisher and Ury argue that positional bargaining does not tend to produce good agreements. It is an inefficient means of reaching agreements, and the agreements tend to neglect the parties' interests. It encourages stubbornness and so tends to harm the parties' relationship. Principled negotiation provides a better way of reaching good agreements. Fisher and Ury's process of principled negotiation can be used effectively on almost any type of dispute. Their four principles are (1) separate the people from the problem; (2) focus on interests rather than positions; (3) generate a variety of options before settling on an agreement; and (4) insist that the agreement be based on objective criteria.

4.   Michelle LeBaron, "Culture-Based Negotiation Styles," July 2003, online   at   <http://www.beyondintractability.org/essay/culture_negotiation/> (as of 2 March 2006).

5.   Mitrovica (2001), 48–50.

6.   Much of this section was derived from Max Smith, "International Business Negotiations: A Comparison of Theory with the Perceived Reality of Australian Practitioners," School of Commerce, the Flinders University of South Australia, Research Paper Series: 00-9, ISSN: 1441-3906, undated. Online at <http://www.ssn.flinders.edu.au/commerce/researchpapers/00–9.doc> (as of 2 March 2006).

7.   Jeswald W. Salacuse, "Ten Ways That Culture Affects Negotiating Style: Some Survey Results," *Negotiation Journal*, July 1998, 223.

8.   Salacuse (1998), 223.

9.   Leszek Buszynski, "Negotiating Styles in the Middle East," *The Practicing Manager*, vol. 13, no. 2, 1993, 20.

10.   Smith, "International Business Negotiations."

11.   LeBaron (2003).

12.   Ibid.

13.   Ibid.

14.   Center for Army Lessons Learned (CALL), "Chapter 2: Civil Military Operations—Civil Affairs, Topic C: Cultural Issues in Iraq," in *Operation Iraqi Freedom (OIF)*, CAAT II Initial Impressions Report (IIR) No. 04-13 (Fort Leavenworth, KS: Center for Army Lessons Learned, May 2004).

15.   Smith, *International Business Negotiations.*

16.   Ibid.

17.   Adapted from Frank L. Acuff, *How to Negotiate with Anyone, Anywhere Around the World*, new expanded ed., New York: AMACOM, 1997.

Appendix D

The Implications of Cultural Factors for
US Operations in Somalia

This appendix discusses the implications of culture for US operations in Somalia during the 1990s. The discussion draws on the cultural awareness factors described in chapter 3.

US Operations in Somalia

On 24 April 1992, the United Nations Operation in Somalia I (UNOSOM I) was established to monitor the cease-fire and to provide protection and security to personnel, equipment, and humanitarian assistance in Mogadishu, Somalia. In August 1992, the UNOSOM I mandate was changed to enable United Nations (UN) forces to protect humanitarian convoys and distribution centers throughout Somalia. On 26 March 1993, as Somalia continued on its path toward lawlessness and anarchy, the UN Security Council established UNOSOM II. This new resolution (UNSCR 814) provided a new mandate allowing UNOSOM II forces to assist the Somali people in rebuilding their economic, political, and social infrastructure with the goal of recreating a democratic Somalia. The main responsibilities of UNOSOM II included monitoring the end of hostilities; preventing renewed violence; seizing unauthorized small arms; maintaining security at seaports, airports, and road networks required for delivery of humanitarian assistance; mine-clearing; and assisting with the return of refugees in Somalia. In February 1994, after several violent incidents and attacks on UN soldiers, the Security Council revised the UNOSOM II mandate and began withdrawing troops and reducing support to UN agencies, human rights organizations, and nongovernmental organizations (NGOs). UNOSOM II completed its withdrawal on 28 March 1995.

The analysis of UNOSOM I and II provides a backdrop for understanding the importance of cultural awareness and competence as it applies to US adversaries and allies as well as NGOs. Although cultural misunderstandings are not the root of all problems besetting conflict, these factors are important and can shed insight on certain aspects of the operation.

Understanding Somali Culture

Many problems faced by the UN throughout the scope of UNOSOM I and II operations can be connected to a failure to understand Somali culture. First, misperception of the Somali clan structure and ignorance of the notion of "collective responsibility" led the coalition to concentrate its attention on Ali Mahdi and Aideed—Somalia's main warlords. The unintended consequence of this was that UN actions actually increased the warlords' degree of power and authority, which was desirable to the warlords but led to the marginalization of other clans, thereby upsetting the traditional balance of the Somali kinship system.[1]

The second failure relates to the difference between western linear approaches to problem solving compared to the "circular" Somali approach.[2] This became even more crucial when the Somali "nomadic" concept of time was ignored in favor of the time-constrained negotiations imposed by the United Nations.[3]

The third failure was a misunderstanding of the Somali oral culture. Even though most of the population could not read, initial information operation campaigns focused on dropping leaflets instead of leveraging the widely available BBC radio to broadcast the aims and policies of the United Nations to the Somali population. These leaflets failed to get the message to the Somali population; moreover, widely publicized images of American helicopters dropping leaflets had a significant negative effect.

The fourth failure concerns the nation's reconciliation process.[4] In Somali society, self-motivated conflict resolution is highly valued, and uninvited intervention by outsiders rarely solves the problem. In contrast to the Western concept of impartiality, Somalis see a third party as untrustworthy. In this environment, top-down approaches are not encouraged. Instead, the local tradition of conflict resolution draws on a variety of local influences and practices:

- Somali moral commonwealth (customary social code).
- Assemblies of elders (responsible for arbitrating conflicts).
- Use of elders as mediators.
- Use of open councils (involvement of women).

Understanding Coalition Cultures

Cultural awareness is not only important to understanding US adversaries—it is also necessary to operate effectively with US allies. During the UNISOM I and II operations, more than thirty nations contributed over 28,000 troops and military personnel. It was inevitable that cultural differences would arise. The three multinational task forces that were created faced many cultural challenges, including:

- Different views and interpretations of peacekeeping operations between Western, Eastern, and African nations.
- Command and control compromises, which had to meet national restrictions and constraints.
- Huge variances in logistics capabilities.
- The differing personalities of the on-scene commanders (i.e., US and Italian commanders) leading to the deterioration of operations development and tempo.

- Diverse languages, leading to poor interoperability and enhanced or amplified pre-existing problems.

A final difference that surfaced concerned multiple interpretations of the rules of engagement (ROE). US troops were more confrontational and more likely to use force, while the European and Australian troops were less confrontational and focused on using the "soft power" of dialogue and mediation. A lack of cultural awareness and competence in Somalia during the conduct of UNISOM I and II created severe tensions between the United States and its allies, and directly impacted the combat effectiveness of the mission and perhaps its ultimate failure.

Understanding Humanitarian Assistance Organizational Cultures

One of the most overlooked problems emerged because of cultural differences between NGOs and the military. These cultural differences, based on distinctly different perspectives, created mutual suspicion and contributed to an unhealthy competition between these organizations. From the beginning, frustrations and misunderstandings arose due to different perceptions of roles and missions. The military believed that its primary responsibility was to provide security and relegated the NGO to a supplemental role of delivering goods and services. The NGOs believed they had the main role of providing services to the Somalis while the military supported them by providing security.

Another area of misunderstanding emerged because of stereotyping. Many in the military felt the NGOs were disorganized, wasteful, inexperienced, liberal, antimilitary, academic, self-righteous, and incompetent, while many in the NGOs felt the military was insensitive, inflexible, conservative, bureaucratic, and obsessive about preventing mission creep.[5]

The different perspectives and stereotyping reduced the effectiveness of the peacekeeping and humanitarian assistance operations on both sides and influenced the overall mission by affecting credibility and decreasing worldwide legitimacy. Criticality of the mission could not afford duplication of efforts. The two components must understand and complement each other beginning in the planning phase.

Notes

1.   Tamara Duffey, "Cultural Issues in Contemporary Peacekeeping," *International Peacekeeping*, vol. 7, no. 1, 2000, 158.

2.   Ibid., 159.

3.   Ibid. Duffey states that Special Representative to Secretary General Mr. Sahnoun took nearly two months to discuss and negotiate with Somali representatives, which led to the Jubaland Peace Agreement. This was contrasted with Sahnoun's replacement, Ismat Kittani, who was ordered out of Somali territory after demanding the Somalis produce a full agreement within 2 hours.

4.   Ibid., 160–162.

5.   Ibid., 156.

About the Author

William D. Wunderle is career Army officer with a wide range of education, training, and experience with regard to the Middle East. He has served in the Joint Strategic Plans and Policy Directorate (J5) on the Joint Staff as a Political Military Planner with responsibility for Iran, Syria, Lebanon, and the Palestinian Authority. Prior assignments include Senior Army Fellow at the RAND Corporation; principal US advisor to the Saudi Arabian Ministry of Defense and Aviation Joint Staff; Chief of Plans, Operations Officer, and infantry company commander with the 82d Airborne Division at Fort Bragg, North Carolina; and Chief of Strategic Plans for US Army South and J3, Joint Security Brigade, Operation Safe Haven. Wunderle served as a consultant for the University of Southern California's Institute for Creative Technologies Enhanced Learning Environments with Creative Technologies (ELECT) project—a PC-based, bilateral contact-training module that allows US Army leaders to plan and conduct a series of bilateral meetings. Wunderle is a non-resident associate at Georgetown's Institute for the Study of Diplomacy and an adjunct instructor for the University of Maryland University College.

Wunderle is a graduate of the Joint and Combined Warfighting Course at the Joint Forces Staff College in Norfolk, Virginia, and the Arabic Basic Course at the Defense Language Institute Foreign Language Center, Presidio of Monterey, California. He holds an MBA from Benedictine College, Atchison, Kansas; an MMAS from the School of Advanced Military Studies, US Army Command and General Staff College, Fort Leavenworth, Kansas; and a BA from Cleveland State University, Cleveland, Ohio.

Wunderle has published a number of books, monographs, and articles, including: "US Foreign Policy and Israel's Qualitative Military Edge: the Need for a Common Vision," with Lt Col Andre Briere, *Policy Focus Series*, the Washington Institute for Near East Policy, January 2008; "Augmenting Israel's Qualitative Military Edge," with Lt Col Andre Briere, *Middle East Quarterly*, Winter 2008, Volume 15, Number 1; "Uncertain Future: A Strategic Review of the Middle East and Implications for the United States," with Andre Briere, National Institute of Public Policy's *Comparative Strategy*, Volume 26, Issue 3, May 2007; "Middle East Negotiation Styles: Preparing for Negotiations in the Middle East," *Military Review*, Fort Leavenworth, Kansas, March–April 2007; *Forced In, Left Out: The Airborne Division in Future Forcible Entry Operations* (Fort Leavenworth, KS: US Army Command and General Staff College, School of Advanced Military Studies, 1997); and "Through the Lens of Cultural Awareness: Planning Requirements in Wielding the Instruments of National Power," RAND Technology and Applied Sciences Group Seminar "Warfighters: Operational Realities," 17 November 2004. His monograph *Yin and Yang: The Relationship of Joint Vision 2010's Concepts of Dominant*

Maneuver and Precision Engagement (Fort Leavenworth, KS: US Army Command and General Staff College, School of Advanced Military Studies, 1998), was selected for further publication and distribution by the Association of the United States Army's Institute of Land Warfare as part of their Contemporary Professional Military Writing Series.